THE PSALMS
IN THE LIFE OF GOD'S PEOPLE

Dermot Cox,

THE PSALMS IN THE LIFE OF GOD'S PEOPLE

St Paul Publications

St Paul Publications
Middlegreen, Slough SL3 6BT, England

First published October 1984
Printed by the Society of St Paul, Slough
ISBN 085439 237 8

St Paul Publications is an activity of the priests and
brothers of the Society of St Paul who promote the Christian
message through the mass media

CONTENTS

INTRODUCTION

No personal relationship is either simple or easy. Human nature obtrudes, and this is particularly true of the intimate relationship that exists between God and the people he has taken to himself in marriage (Jer 2,2). It is this interplay of personality between a God who speaks and an individual who listens (and talks back) that characterizes the psalms, for they are a living record of human intercourse with God.

One problem is the fact that the psalter has played such a large part in the prayer-life of Jew and Christian alike — and for so long — that it is easy to forget there is more to it than prayer. It is primarily *God*'s word, an act of self-communication. But it is also the poetic expression of man's experience of that act, and represents the way a particular individual understood the event and reacted to it. The primacy of revelation, then, adds a new dimension to the prayer of Israel, old and new, for the one who listens — the reader — not only learns what God has to say, he also learns how God wished him to respond. The desire to establish communion of life is a divine initiative. What this means is that for a covenant-people prayer is a question of mutuality and so is not without the tensions inherent in any personal relationship, for both God and man make demands on each other. This dialogue structure dominates the psalms. They reflect the whole range of attitudes that make up an individual's approach to God, and so the reader enters upon a personal adventure, growing in knowledge and intimacy as he shares the experiences of individuals rather like himself who probe the mystery of life and discover, not only the many faces of the divinity, but their own humanity before God.

As prayer in poetic form the psalms are best understood in their *personal* context. Seen as individual units, each one is found to be one human being's response to life as it is experienced. It is in the arena of real life that God speaks to man, and the strength of the psalter lies in the fact that it represents a very concrete human reaction to a known divine initiative. So behind the poetic record one can hear the echo of the divine voice that provoked the response. Through the poetry of the psalter one meets religious people who have themselves encountered God on ground common to all: the permanent invalid (Ps 88) and the old (Ps 71); those who mourn (Ps 6) and those who rejoice (Ps 147); those who fear for their faith (Ps 73) and those who are secure (Ps 136). Even the coward (Ps 31) finds his own voice in the psalms.

They were, after all, written with a reader in mind, and through them every reader can share an experience of God and so come to an awareness of what this means for him in terms of a personal response to a living God. For faith, as it is understood by these poets, is less a doctrine *about* God than an intimacy with him based on encounter.

ACKNOWLEDGEMENTS

Weiser, A., *The Psalms. A Commentary.*
London, S.C.M. Press, 1962.

Dahood, M., *Psalms* (Anchor Bible), 3 vols.
New York, Doubleday, 1965–70.

Drijvers, P., *The Psalms. Their Structure and Meaning.*
London, Burns & Oates, 1965.

Ringgren, H., *The Faith of the Psalmists.*
London, S.C.M. Press, 1963.

Ackroyd, P. R., *Doors of Perception, a Guide to Reading the Psalms.*
London, S.C.M. Press, 1983.

Alonso Schökel, L., *The Inspired Word.*
New York, Herder & Herder, 1965.

Buber, M., *Good and Evil.*
New York, Charles Scribner's Sons, 1953.

Rad, G. von, *Old Testament Theology*, 2 vols.
Edinburgh, Oliver & Boyd, 1965.

The Scripture quotations in this publication are from the Revised Standard Version of the Bible, copyrighted 1946, 1952 © 1971, 1973 by the Division of Christian Education of the National Council of the Churches of Christ in the U.S.A., and used by permission.

CHAPTER 1

THE PRAYER OF THE PEOPLE OF GOD

Familiarity too often transforms truth into stereotype. This contributes to the fact that the psalms, being perhaps the most familiar part of the Old Testament, are seldom seen for what they really are, and even less frequently interrogated by a reader in search of meaning. He presumes he knows them; they are part of his tradition. But the originality of poetry is often lost when it is anthologized, and that happened to the poetic heritage of Israel when the psalms were assembled between the covers of a book and labelled 'Psalter'. The passion and grief of a whole people was institutionalized.

Once restore them to their original human context, however, and they may be seen for what they really are: the living voice of a race, expressive of all the passion, grief and love humanity can generate. For the collection of lyrics, laments and invective that comes under the heading of 'Psalms' represents the vital spirit of the Old Testament, and each poem represents a single moment of heightened sensibility and an insight into life.

The Psalms in Perspective

When one of these poems is replaced in its natural ambient and seen with fresh eyes its spirit can be apprehended more intensely, its inner nature understood. Set thus against its own individual background it may speak for itself. In the *Book of Exodus* one short passage stands in a special relationship to its surroundings:

> Then Moses and the people of Israel sang this song to the Lord,
> saying,
> 'I will sing to the Lord, for he has triumphed gloriously;
> the horse and his rider he has thrown into the sea.
> The Lord is my strength and my song, and he has become my
> salvation;
> this is my God, and I will praise him,
> my father's God, and I will exalt him.
> The Lord is a man of war;
> the Lord is his name'.
>
> (Ex 15, 1–3)

This poem is characteristic of a particular style of writing. While it purports to be the 'voice of Moses', his 'psalm of thanksgiving', it can equally well represent the voice of Israel many generations later, for it expresses, simply and vividly, both a believer's understanding of a single divine intervention and his human response to it. Something has happened to Moses and his followers that sparked a *verbal reaction* at once immediate and transcendent.

In fact, many such individual poems have escaped the editorial hand of the anthologist and for that reason draw attention to what a 'psalm' is all about in its own right. Some, like Ex 15, are familiar by reason of frequent liturgical usage but there are others, such as the 'Song of Jonah' from Jon 2,3–9 and the exultant 'Song of Hannah' in 1 Sam 2,1–10. In all of these the context in life (as it is represented) serves to highlight the inner nature of a psalm, which is clearly seen to be the expression in poetic form of a human reaction to a divine intervention. In the case of 1 Sam 2 the fact that Hannah's cry of triumph is clearly a later composition than the story in the book, and is moreover expressive of a community reaction as much as that of an individual, shows how the reality that triggered the response transcended the narrow limits of private experience and historical time. Hannah's personal experience of divine intervention could serve a later generation as a blueprint for national salvation, since God's promptness to act was as real for the community as it had been for her. In a real sense, every psalm can be understood as a human response to a divine act, and this marks all of biblical prayer with a special character.

The Nature of Biblical Religion

The world of the psalms is a world in which God seeks man. *He* takes the initiative, and it is his 'word' that creates the hearer's reply. The polarity of positive and negative that marks so many psalms (as 30 and 119) represents the real crisis that is inherent in such dialogue, for it presents a God who offers himself — and may be refused. Acceptance of a divine initiative is always an option. Thus the very nature of a psalm is a reminder of one basic fact: that biblical prayer cannot be divorced from a concrete response to a call, since the faith of the psalmist is an attitude of response to a personal experience of encounter that is actualized in the recitation of the psalm. Ps 95 ends with a warning that is as real to first century Israel as it was centuries earlier at Sinai: 'if you hearken to my voice *today* . . . you will experience theophany' (v. 7d). The 'today' of this challenge is as real a moment of crisis for every successive generation in Israel as the Sinai experience had been for Moses and his companions. This in fact is the function of v. 7 as it stands in the text:

> For he is our God,
>   and we are the people of his pasture,
>   and the sheep of his hand.
> O that today you would hearken to his voice!

In the first part of this verse the recitation of the covenant-formula in poetic form — 'he is our God, and we the people of his pasture, and the sheep of his hand' — is the motivation for the response of the community (vv. 8–11) to the divine encounter that marked the first half of the psalm (vv. 2–7c).

In this way, the relationship between Israel and God is a matter of reciprocity. God presents himself in an act of deliverance and the believer responds in praise. Similarly, in suffering the individual raises a lament (secure in his historical perception of Yahweh) and God intervenes to save. Even the frequent joy of the psalmist is a response to a divine grace of existence. Thus the psalms are always a form of dialogue with a divinity who makes himself present; and because of this, in the movement of prayer one finds the face of God. The psalms become an arena of encounter and so the source of religious attitudes. They show how God wishes to invade a human life, and they lay down the parameters of response. The psalter is primarily a divine word of self-communication, so while the formal structure may be that of prayer or praise the essential nature of the genre is *revelation.* God has spoken before ever man can respond, and in his word has already suggested the language of human response.

This fact is crucial to any real understanding of the role of the psalms in the life of the reader. They cannot be solely, or primarily, a subjective or 'affective' prayer, for their nature as revelation is integral to them and brands them ineluctably as an answer to a definite statement. Thus the relationship they inaugurate is with a *known* person — God, and within established categories. For Israel the prayer of the psalms was, like all human encounter, a matter of responding to and learning about another person. Psalmody is theologically dominated by dialogue-structure, representing as it does a divine intervention (of redemption or creation) and a human reaction. This underpins the nature of the psalms as essentially *divine revelation in prayer form.* Their immediate purpose is to promote a relationship between the reader and God, based on what God has offered or is offering by means of his word. The nature of Old Testament prayer must always be borne in mind: a suppliant realistically accepting a relationship to his God, being well aware of the fact that this is going to make demands on him.

If the psalms thus represent a response to God's initiative, it follows that many of them become a personal search for the meaning of that divine act, an attempt at 'seeing his face'. For example, in Ps 95 and Ps 105 one meets the divine intervention of Exodus, yet the *prayer* of either psalm is effectively an enquiry into the meaning of Exodus, not just in history *but now in the suppliant's life situation.* So one further dimension is added to their significance: while ostensibly they may deal with one or other episode in Israel's history they become for each reader parables of human experience, eternally fresh and valid:

> When evildoers assail me,
> uttering slanders against me,
> my adversaries and foes,
> they shall stumble and fall.
> Though a host encamp against me,
> my heart shall not fear;
> though war arise against me,
> yet I will be confident.
>
> (Ps 27,2–3)

By re-living, now, a 'then' experience one can find the means of transcending it, finding meaning, starting afresh in life — for the God who acted once can act again! Theologically, revelation is frequently a record of God's search for man. And because the psalms are thus divine 'word' in prayer-form, *prayer becomes sacrament*, and effects encounter and response at the level of everyday life.

The Psalms as Sacrament

The abiding theme of the psalter is the continually renewed encounter of God and his people in saving acts. Their theology was both historical and logical. The historical basis of faith was the Sinai

Covenant, which had ended with a divine guarantee of God's 'presence' to Israel's need (Ex 23,20–33). Logically, it followed that since Exodus had been the great 'saving' event of Israel's history it would remain effective in the people's need. Yet it had happened once, a long time ago for a different generation — how then could it be real to a Jew of the Exile period, or later? The answer is to be found in the concept of 'word and event', or better still 'word re-creating experience', as it might be called. The question is — what is the biblical manner of passing on religious commitment to a new generation?

The Bible, in fact, does not set out to provide a systematic 'deposit' of doctrine about man, world or God; nor does it communicate abstract propositions or *beliefs about* doctrine or morals. God's self-revelation in the Old Testament is a progressive series of interventions in time that thrusts towards an eschatological terminus. Internally, it involves an appropriation of the *meaning* and *value* of each event as this is re-experienced by means of recitation. The nature of God cannot be presented abstractly. He can be known as, year after year, Israel liturgically re-experiences a particular event by which he communicates himself. Having been known in this way, the experience can be expanded by an explanation of what has happened to the reader or reciter. The classic text in this regard must surely be Josh 24 — the so-called 'Sinai Covenant sacrament' or the 'Covenant renewal sacrament'. An analysis of the text makes the theological principle of *word effecting experience* quite clear.

It deals formally with second-generation Israelites — the first generation having died out in the wilderness along with Moses. So Joshua is represented as addressing a people who (for the most part, at least) had never had the personal experience of God that Sinai had been; and more, it may be inferred from the context that the Shechemites — a pagan people — also form part of the congregation. Yet this heterogeneous audience takes on all the implications and obligations of a covenant — that same Covenant their fathers had made as a result of an experience at Sinai forty years in the past. The stylistic parallel of 'your fathers' (i.e. 'then') and 'you' (i.e. 'now') is deliberate. Compare v. 2b with v. 14a, and v. 15a with 15b:

> Then Joshua gathered all the tribes of Israel to Shechem, and summoned the elders, the heads, the judges, and the officers of Israel; and they presented themselves before God. And Joshua

> said to all the people, 'Thus says the Lord, the God of Israel, "Your fathers lived of old beyond the Euphrates, Terah, the father of Abraham and of Nahor; and they served other gods . . ."
>
> 'Now therefore fear the Lord, and serve him in sincerity and in faithfulness; put away the gods which your fathers served beyond the River, and in Egypt, and serve the Lord. And if you be unwilling to serve the Lord, choose this day whom you will serve, whether the gods your fathers served in the region beyond the River, or the gods of the Amorites in whose land you dwell; but as for me and my house, we will serve the Lord'.

And it is very noticeable that Joshua's imperative, found here in v. 15, is 'choose *this day*' what your response is to be. It may therefore be inferred that the new generation (and those among the pagans who may choose to do so) makes an individual decision *on the basis of the experience of the Sinai redemptive act*; an act that is now 'sacramentally' communicated *by means of the recitation, the 'word', of that experience* found in vv. 2b–13. What has happened is that a totally 'new' group of people 'learned their faith', not by instruction, but by experiencing in their own lives the objective reality of a redemptive event re-enacted by recitation, by 'word'. And thus by means of a 'recitative word' the reality of the Sinai experience (of the past) becomes a reality to be experienced in the present; and this experience of God elicits a response that is 'faith'.

That this is a common biblical concept is borne out by two other texts from the Old Testament canon, Deut 5,3 and 26,5–9, where we learn that the Sinai Covenant *is made with us readers*, for we are direct participators in that historical situation: 'and behold, now, *I* bring the first of the fruit of the ground, which you, O Lord, have given me' (Deut 26,10).

The recitation of a psalm was more than an act of remembrance. It inserted the reader into the reality of a divine act of liberation. The above texts from *Joshua* and *Deuteronomy* are by no means isolated phenomena. Ps 100 functions in a similar way. Here in v. 2 a phrase is used that echoes throughout the psalter: 'come into his presence . . . with singing'. This is more than a metaphor, as the original phrase in Hebrew implies. God was thought of as actually there, his presence evoked by the act of 'singing' or recital. This had been guaranteed by Sinai. And not only was he present, he was present as an effective and saving God. The very structure of the psalm emphasises this idea. The invitation to come 'face to face' with God in vv. 2–3 leads into the hymn proper, vv. 3–4 with its emphatic declaration:

Know that the Lord is God!
It is he that made us, and we are his;
we are his people, and the sheep of his pasture.
Enter his gates with thanksgiving,
and his courts with praise!
Give thanks to him, bless his name!

The motive clause in v. 3, with its poetic re-echo of the covenant formula ('I will walk among you, and will be your God, and you shall be my people', Lev 26,12), recalls the special relationship between Yahweh and Israel that resulted from the Sinai experience, and it serves as the basis of the confidence expressed. Verse 4 is a re-statement in slightly different terms of the invitation of v. 2, emphasizing in its turn the motive for praise and thanksgiving.

If one can imagine, between v. 2a and vv. 2b–4, the implied question 'how?' one will have a clearer grasp of what is happening: an invitation to come into the presence of God (v. 2a) is followed by a question as to how this might be done; the response is 'by means of recitation' ('with singing', v. 2b), and an evocation of the Sinai experience follows (v. 3) by way of confirmation. This whole process is nailed in place by a new injunction to recite what is obviously a psalm of entrance to the liturgy (v. 4). An act of faith in the enduring nature of God's concern for his covenant people closes the hymn very effectively:

his steadfast love endures forever,
and his faithfulness to all generations!

To the Israelite, the fact of Yahweh's presence to them in psalmody was a very real thing. Effectively, it was a tenet of faith. It meant that redemption itself was a fact, not just of history, but in their own 'today' (as Ps 95,7d is careful to emphasize). Also, this presence in some way implied the presence of his entire salvific work in that history. Through the act of recitation this presence now exercises its influence. Ps 81 clearly suggests this:

Sing aloud to God our strength;
shout for joy to the God of Jacob!
Raise a song, sound the timbrel, the sweet lyre with the harp.

Blow the trumpet at the new moon, at the full moon, on our feast
day.
For it is a statute for Israel, an ordinance of the God of Jacob.
He made it a decree in Joseph, when he went out over the land of
Egypt.

I hear a voice I had not known:
'I relieved your shoulder of the burden;
your hands were freed from the basket.
In distress you called, and I delivered you;
I answered you in the secret place of thunder;
I tested you at the waters of Meribah'.

From even a preliminary reading one thing is very clear — a change in thrust that becomes evident after v. 5b. The 'voice I had not known' of v. 5c is that of God himself, and it signals the divine oracle (pronounced by a priest or liturgical leader, perhaps) that follows from v. 6 to v. 16. Thus it forms a bridge between the first five verses of summons to prayer and the result of this invitation, the second part of the psalm that is marked by a change from third person to second, and a shift to the present tense as the hearer, one of a new generation in Israel, is personally involved in the historical event: 'in distress *you* called, and I (Yahweh) delivered *you*', releasing your shoulder of the burden and your hand from the basket (Exodus terminology); and so it is *you* that is *now* challenged by the Meribah event (vv. 6,7a and 7b). The rest of the psalm reiterates the need for a personal response (vv. 8–9) based on the effectiveness of the historical Exodus-event in the 'now' of the hearer — 'I am the Lord your God, who brought you up out of the land of Egypt. Open your mouth wide, and I will fill it' (v. 10). It is clear from the opening verses of this psalm that cultic recital becomes a sacrament of encounter, remembrance of the redemptive deeds of liberation in the Exodus from Egypt effecting the insertion of the hearer into the reality of that act. Thus worship is not merely the *result* of religious experience — it also creates it anew, so that a common experience (such as that of the Red Sea deliverance or the Sinai covenant) becomes each worshipper's own experience.

For Israel, then, the prayer of the psalms served to preserve the continuity of her great religious experience in the Exodus, when redemption was effected. Now this event is seen for what it is — not just an experience her forefathers had enjoyed, but one that every generation may have in its turn. Each time Israel recited these psalms in the liturgy she appropriated to herself the redeeming work of Yahweh, and on the basis of that encounter made her own response. Ps 18 presents another aspect of this belief:

> I love thee, O Lord, my strength.
> The Lord is my rock, and my fortress, and my deliverer,
> my God, my rock, in whom I take refuge,
> my shield, and the horn of my salvation, my stronghold.
> I call upon the Lord, who is worthy to be praised,
> and I am saved from my enemies.
> The cords of death encompassed me, the torrents of perdition assailed me;
> the cords of Sheol entangled me, the snares of death confronted me.
>
> (vv. 1–5)

This is a royal thanksgiving for divine aid given in time of need (found also in 2 Sam 22). One notes how, after the initial introductory phrase in v. 2, the style changes from confession to narrative. The use of the 'present tense' (in Hebrew implying continuity) serves to make the past events being recorded actual in the present situation of the one who recites the psalm — possibly a monarch fresh from a victory in battle, for whom God's *past* act of mighty liberation (possibly the Red Sea crossing), being evoked, has now turned the day (see vv. 34ff). The 'act of God' in question is described in vv. 7–19 in terms of a theophany. Some interpreters see this as a description of a thunderstorm, but perhaps this is to naturalize it too much. The imagery is mixed, and recalls both the Red Sea liberation (from Ex 14) and the Sinai theophany (from Ex 19,16) — the two as it were becoming one mighty act of warlike delivery. So it is likely that it serves here as a literary device — the use of imagery to communicate the liberation experience of Israel. This results in the psalmist reliving the Exodus experience, as the past event becomes effective once again for him.

The Importance of the Concept for Judaism

This 'sacramental' belief was crucial to worship both in the psalter and in later Judaism. In the text of Ex 12,40–42 and in the Targum one can find a Jewish approach to recitation that influenced the prayer-life of God's people in the Old Testament, and that was certainly known in the Palestine of the first century A.D.

Ex 12,40–42 itself consists of a simple historical introduction (v. 40), followed by a memorial of the Passover (v. 41) and a theologico-liturgical interpretation of that event (it was 'a night of watching by the Lord', v. 42a). All of this is rounded off by what is clearly a ritual injunction to repeat this act of prayer time and again (it is 'to be kept to the Lord by all the people of Israel *throughout their generations*', v. 42b). The Palestinian Targum, serving as a liturgical paraphrase and commentary on Ex 12, presents a striking theological development of this text in a poem entitled 'Four Nights', a kind of celebration in four acts, in which four stages of saving history are presented — from Creation through the call of Abraham to the Egyptian Passover — the whole culminating, on the fourth night, in a 'Pasch of the World'. This represented the time of the Messiah, when all of these salvific events would, cumulatively, be actualized as the salvation of God. The liturgical celebration thus depicted resulted in the recitation of the event becoming the resonance, the 're-sounding', and actualization of the 'word' which involved the hearer in a 'today' situation. All of this expresses a belief in the continuity of divine intervention, as the echo of the divine word resounds through the ages and so becomes part of the present of those who hear the recitation, leading them to insert themselves into the actual event and its implications (see Lk 4 and Acts 13,5).

This consequence of personal responsibility is crucial. In all biblical worship one can perceive two constituent parts — a divine action or intervention, and a human response to that. The same polarity is found in the psalms. Each time the psalmist prays, he encounters God in the history of what he did to redeem him (thus actualizing Exodus), and on his own part he responds to this initiative. A simple break-down of the structure of Ps 59 makes this clear:

vv. 1–7: the prayer of the psalmist.
vv. 8–10: an act of faith.
vv. 11–17: a cry for vindication.

The prayer of the psalmist depicting his actual situation — one of need, for the psalm is formally a 'Lament' — includes an appeal to Yahweh's saving power as God of Sabaoth and warrior-king of Israel who has already 'proved himself' historically by dispossessing the nations in favour of his people:

Thou, Lord God of hosts, art God of Israel.
Awake to punish all the nations;
spare none of those who treacherously plot evil.
(v. 5)

This 'act of recital' is followed by the expected epiphany of God acting according to his true nature as one who has always been 'present to his people in their need' (cf. Ex 3 and Lev 26,12). In the central section, from v. 8 to v. 10, the last verse represents a moment of encounter as God intervenes in answer to the confident prayer of his suppliant:

But thou, O Lord, dost laugh at them;
thou dost hold all the nations in derision.
O my Strength, I will sing praises to thee;
for thou, O God, art my fortress.
My God in his steadfast love will meet me;
my God will let me look in triumph on my enemies.

After an appeal for vengeance there follows the psalmist's reaction in vv. 16–17 — an act of testimony:

But I will sing of thy might;
I will sing aloud of thy steadfast love in the morning.
For thou hast been to me a fortress and a refuge in the day of my distress.
O my Strength, I will sing praises to thee,
for thou, O God, art my fortress,
the God who shows me steadfast love.

Even allowing for the obscurity of much of this highly stylized poem, certain things stand out clearly. Framed by a description of the actual life-situation of the psalmist (vv. 3–4 and vv. 16b–17 represent the 'before and after', as it were), a recital of God's saving acts results in a moment of encounter, and this is followed by a human response of praise and witness. In fact, the psalm has become, in one sense, a theophany of God manifesting himself to a suppliant and that individual responding.

In its own way, moreover, this attitude of response is *mutual*. Because it is a commitment on man's part it is also, on the part of God, an act of *claiming* his people as his own, restoring the covenant relationship. He 'puts his name' on them (as in Num 6,27), imposing to some degree his nature upon man who thereby becomes sacred — a participator in the divine. In this way the psalms continually renew the encounter of God and his people. When Israel recited, she renewed an act of God in her own personal history and made that commitment, which had long before been accepted by Moses and his followers, her own personal commitment. As always, recital involved both challenge and acceptance.

The Dramatization of Encounter and Response

The radical nature of this option is borne out by a type of psalm (elements of which have been seen in Ps 59 above) that deals with God's 'vengeance' or 'anger' — the so-called 'cursing psalms' such as 58,6ff, and 137,8ff. More often than not this is a literary *dramatization* of the human situation of the psalmist. They represent human beings in a state of tension. Contemporary readers might think that such excessive expression of man's lower nature had no place in his conversation with God, but to the man of the Old Testament this scarcely posed a problem. The psalms represent human speech; they are voices from the arena of real life where individuals are less than perfect and so capable of anger, even of vindictiveness. It is on this realistic level that the psalmist wants to meet God and speak to him. And the fact of human limitation, no less than the poet's eye of realism in art, almost makes anger a necessary part of any life lived between God and his creature. This fact is compounded by the terrestrial boundaries set to the human project in the Old Testament. Death was the end of all relationships, so they had to be understood in terms of this world; and if God were called on to intervene *in favour* of an oppressed innocent, he logically had to intervene *against* the oppressor. Naturally, the more personally felt the offence, the more vigorously expressed was the desire for vindication. But what is intended is the divine act of salvation — the logical corollary adds a touch of realism and poetic colour. From the artistic point of view — which is that of the writer — there is no doubt that anger and vindictiveness are potent symbols of human response. Who can blame the poets of the Old Testament for immediately seeing the dramatic possibilities? So, in these psalms of vengeance, the two clearly distinguished poles of 'good' and 'bad', black and white, can be understood as a symbolic designation of man faced with an option.

By means of the recitation of a psalm, an actual situation of encounter is presented and the response depends on each individual.

If one chooses to go the 'way of evildoers' (Ps 1), then the consequences are of one's own making, *and they are grave*, for the choice is radical — one of life and death, not just for oneself but for the community to which one becomes either a power for good or a living cancer to be ruthlessly excised. The dramatic highlighting of this situation by commination or vow of vengeance serves to underline the critical nature of the choice and the fact that a faith-response is an option, *and may be refused*. In the psalm a drama of redemption is presented, and experienced, as something *exigent*. This is not to say that many psalms do not exhibit a real element of vindictiveness — but this also serves to underline the very humanity of the poet: to him God was so real that any refusal of divine self-giving was heinous beyond reasoning.

Indeed, Ps 7 reflects this notion in an unusual way, becoming as it were a 'reversed' cursing psalm:

O Lord my God, in thee do I take refuge;
save me from all my pursuers, and deliver me,
lest like a lion they rend me, dragging me away, with none to rescue.

O Lord my God, if I have done this, if there is wrong in my hands,
if I have requited my friend with evil or plundered my enemy without cause,
let the enemy pursue me and overtake me,
and let him trample my life to the ground,
and lay my soul in the dust.

In these first five verses the 'cursing' element has become a very striking cry of innocence, a poet's dramatization of his own integrity before God and his consequently urgent need of rehabilitation. And vv. 14–17 show its role in the working-out of the dynamic of act-consequence, or retribution:

Behold, the wicked man conceives evil,
and is pregnant with mischief, and brings forth lies.
He makes a pit, digging it out,
and falls into the hole which he has made.
His mischief returns upon his own head,
and on his own pate his violence descends.

I will give to the Lord the thanks due to his righteousness,
and I will sing praise to the name of the Lord, the Most High.

The psalm has become a dramatized evocation of the urgency of the challenge that encounter with God entails, and the moral turpitude of the one who chooses perversely. The fact that they also show the evil of being God's enemy (and therefore Israel's) in terms of good contemporary war propaganda serves as a vivid reminder of the evil one finds in oneself as much as of the radical implications of human choice.

One further perception that lies behind 'dramatization' is the fact that the psalms are meant to express, in poetic form, the tension inherent in man's existence in a world he did not create or choose to inhabit. Thus the genre bears eloquent witness to man's sense of alienation in an absurd cosmos where all men are strangers and anger becomes an expression of selfhood.

The Unity of Salvation-history

It is necessary to understand just how biblical man perceived the history he was living out. He saw it as a series of redemptive events, interventions made by God in time and place that decisively determined the thrust of existence. The past was the spring of Israel's present. Thus all biblical history is marked by a permanent tension, a dynamic of expectation and fulfilment, in which the Old Testament — and thus the psalms — represents a preparatory and provisional stage.

So the psalms, as indeed the prayer-life of Israel as a whole, originate not in speculation *about* God but in a certainty of his historical presence among them, in their lives. This experience of God makes of the psalms a prayer in and for the actual life-situation of the suppliant, and establishes the fact that personal 'faith' is never something inherited, but always a personal commitment made on the basis of an experience of God. This, of course, determines to some extent the meaning of a psalm. It is always a question of encounter, and if one thereby learns *about* God it is always experiential knowledge. The faith of the psalmist rests on fact: God had (once) heard a people in their distress (Ex 3,7ff) and responded to their need (Ex 14). Theologically, he is a God of presence (Ex 3) — the one who is always with his people. 'Presence-to-save' is his nature. And it is in this way that Ps 95 presents him to the reader:

> O that today you would hearken to his voice!
> Harden not your hearts, as at Meribah,
> as on the day at Massah in the wilderness,

when your fathers tested me,
and put me to the proof, though they had seen my work.
For forty years I loathed that generation
and said, 'They are a people who err in heart,
and they do not regard my ways'.
Therefore I swore in my anger that they should not enter my rest.
(vv. 7d–11)

The Wilderness experience depicted in this second half of the psalm was theologically a paradigm of living faith: an ideal, and the human reality; the imperative of faith (v. 7d), and the response — historically a very qualified one (vv. 8–9, which reflect Num 10–12), but still open to a more wholehearted generosity on the part of later generations. The period of desert wandering in Num 10–12 was a parable to later generations, presenting an option to every successive age; for while man's response could vary, God's will to redeem remained constant. He is a God who turns towards man, historically the one who takes the first step in the relationship. He made a promise, and *he kept it*; in his initial approach to Moses he promised to be with his people on their journey (Ex 3,17ff, 'and I promise that I will bring you up out of the affliction of Egypt, to the land of the Canaanites . . . '), and in the course of this journey he proved faithful to that promise (Ex 20,2, 'I am the Lord your God, who brought you out of the land of Egypt, out of the house of bondage'). He remains the same, one whose presence to every generation is effective of human liberation, if they accept the offer. It is in this context that one can understand the psalms as moments in that history shared between God and his covenant people.

The Human Dimension

Apart from their theological value as 'word' of self-revelation, it is evident that the psalms have a particular value as human expressions of joy, sorrow and fear that originated as integral parts of saving-history. They are clearly human voices concurrent with that economy of salvation. Anything that happens in life may thus become a means of encounter, for it will force the individual to turn to God in search of meaning. Thus prayer becomes an arena in which God and man meet to discuss man's affairs. The background of some psalms reflects this, especially the 'songs of ascent', or pilgrimage psalms, though it is not exclusive to these. Indeed, much of the psalter reflects a 'workaday' atmosphere that is refreshing:

> I was glad when they said to me,
>   'Let us go to the house of the Lord!
> Our feet have been standing
>   within your gates, O Jerusalem!
>
> Jerusalem, built as a city which is bound firmly together,
> to which the tribes go up, the tribes of the Lord,
> as was decreed for Israel,
>   to give thanks to the name of the Lord.
> There thrones for judgment were set,
>   the thrones of the house of David.
>
> Pray for the peace of Jerusalem!
>   'May they prosper who love you!
> Peace be within your walls,
>   and security within your towers!'
>
> For my brethren and companions' sake
>   I will say, 'Peace be within you!'
> For the sake of the house of the Lord our God,
>   I will seek your good.
>
> (Ps 122,1–9)

Psalm 122, as one can see, is a psalm of ascent. In a mood that combines the twin spirits of pilgrimage and excursion one 'goes up' to the house of God, in the company of family, friends and fellow-travellers, all of whom share one conviction — that they *belong* there. In a sense they are 'going home'. So, naturally, 'invocation' is followed by a 'prayer' that is expressive of one's everyday need of God and assurance of meeting him. The structure of Ps 121 is as simple as that:

> I lift up my eyes to the hills.
>   From whence does my help come?
> My help comes from the Lord,
>   who made heaven and earth.
> He will not let your foot be moved,
>   he who keeps you will not slumber.
> Behold, he who keeps Israel
>   will neither slumber nor sleep.
>
> (vv. 1–4)

The message is not far to seek: God *is* — that is his nature; and so he acts — to create, to save, to respond even to the most pedestrian of human needs. He keeps 'your going out and your coming in' (Ps 121,8); he gives prosperity to all, 'peace within your walls, and security within your towers' (Ps 122,6–8). And the phrase 'God *is* your help' is almost a refrain (Ps 121,1.5.8; 124,8; 125,2; 130,7) and is certainly a conviction too commonplace to be questioned, let alone proved. These psalms do not restrict prayer to the more important side of religion — for prayer is an expression of life, and that is often humdrum indeed:

> I do not occupy myself with things
> too great and too marvellous for me.
> But I have calmed and quieted my soul,
> like a child quieted at its mother's breast;
> like a child that is quieted is my soul.
> (Ps 131,1b–2)

Elsewhere, the same 'everyday' voices may be heard, even in the most unexpected corners of the psalter. Ps 119 is a very artificial, and even more protracted, 'university lecture' — 176 verses of an acrostic! And like Ps 1 it reflects a later and more legalistic view of Torah religion. Yet behind the dry academic one can sense the dedicated teacher leading a favourite pupil in a common effort at reflection on the nature of divine wisdom. From study comes prayer, a direct dialogue with Wisdom himself — and the formal 'he' of Torah becomes the familiar 'you' of direct intercourse. Even a piece of official versification like Ps 119 suddenly glows from within, and the author can no longer restrain himself:

> I will praise you with an upright heart,
> *when I learn* your ordinances.
> (v. 7)

From meditation has come *recognition* — right there in the lecture hall.

That is often the most striking fact about this poetry. Originating as it often does 'on the street', in the daily experience of life, it testifies to the presence of God on that street, and both 'street' and 'God' are realities, not concepts, to the reader, drawing him into dialogue *now* without need of formal postures. It reflects the actuality of human life whenever or wherever it is lived. Ps 34 confidently records a personal experience, but the sureness of its touch is due to the fact that the author knows his readers will readily identify with the situation, for all are brothers under the skin:

O magnify the Lord with me,
  and let us exalt his name together!
I sought the Lord, and he answered *me* . . .
  So *you* look to him, and be radiant;
  for your face shall never be ashamed.
(vv. 3–5)

Psalm 88 is a more painful comment on human alienation, being the lament of a life-long invalid. But how clearly the human accents come across, in no way impaired by the disparity of time and space, and how perceptible the pain to every reader:

O Lord, my God, I call for help by day;
I cry out at night before thee.
Let my prayer come before thee,
  incline thy ears to my cry!

Afflicted and close to death from youth up,
  I suffer thy terrors; I am helpless.

Thou hast caused lover and friend to shun me;
  my companions are in darkness.
(vv. 1–2, 15, 18)

That particular drama is never played out. Ps 88 is perhaps unique among Laments in that there is no answer from God. True dialogue is absent, for one interlocutor remains inexplicably silent. But perhaps no answer is necessary, for through the act of praying that divine silence meaning has come into a specific situation of human distress.

No, the psalter is not 'a book', except by virtue of the redactor's art. It is a collection of poems by different people in different situations; one hundred and fifty reactions to that common journey all must make from birth to death. As such it embodies one great biblical insight: that holiness is ultimately *this* common life as it actually comes; a reality, not a project. It belongs, therefore, 'on the street' and not between the covers of a book, for the psalms are perceptibly human voices raised in recognition of the ultimate relevance of God to the human situation.

CHAPTER 2

ENCOUNTER AS THE BASIS OF FAITH

In the Old Testament faith was experiential, built up step by step in a series of divine encounters. Communal faith was based on the experiences of Abraham, Moses and the Patriarchs; individual faith on a personal renewal and apperception of those experiences. All of these acts of encounter can broadly be classified as 'gift', or divine initiative; and thus 'faith', whether communal or individual, is seen to be a human reaction to that gift. Israel did not come to a knowledge of God by reason or philosophy. She experienced him, for the God of the Bible is essentially a God who reveals himself, not one who is found or discovered. Man can come to know him primarily by meeting him, and for this reason man's religious attitude is always existential.

Yet the discovery of God in the psalter is not a single experience. It may very well begin with that, as the experience of a particular aspect of God — his purpose of liberation, his creative will, his desire for a relationship — but this is no more than the spark in the stubble. What follows is an ongoing process, as man discovers, one after the other, the many faces of the divine. And so the human 'yes' is itself multi-faceted, to the extent that the single word 'faith' is inadequate to communicate the complexity of the response. No single Hebrew word replaces it in the psalms, for they reveal a many sided human attitude of reaction to a many sided experience of the divine. The basic approach to understanding what the word 'faith' implies must be an awareness of history as a dynamic of divine act and human response; history as an arena in which God acts and may be perceived. When one speaks of a historical saving event in the Old Testament it does not mean 'historical' only in the sense that it happened once *in history*; it is historical also in the sense that it is being continually re-enacted and *is now happening.* The theological perception of God is that he is 'Yahweh' — presence to save. Thus self-revelation and discovery are central to biblical religion, but they are not distinct 'actions' or approaches; one is a catechesis for the other, unleashing its potential: divine presentation of self evoking human knowledge.

Confession of Faith in the Psalms

Scattered throughout the psalter are a number of formal 'credos', essentially poetic and liturgical re-statements of Deut 26,5–10 where the personal experience of God in Exodus becomes concretized in confessional form:

> And you shall make response before the Lord your God, 'A wandering Aramaean was my father; and he went down into Egypt and sojourned there, few in number; and there he became a nation, great, mighty, and populous. And the Egyptians treated us harshly, and afflicted us, and laid upon us hard bondage. Then we cried to the Lord the God of our fathers, and the Lord heard our voice, and saw our affliction, our toil, and our oppression; and the Lord brought us out of Egypt with a mighty hand and an outstretched arm, with great terror, with signs and wonders; and he brought us into this place and gave us this land, a land flowing with milk and honey. And behold, now I bring the first of the fruit of the ground, which thou, O Lord, hast given me.' And you shall set it down before the Lord your God, and worship before the Lord your God.

This remains the basic confession of faith for every successive generation in Israel, whatever the modalities of expression it finds. Three such 'acts of faith' in poetic form are Ps 136, Ps 89 and Ps 135 which present, not a *subjective* experience (as is usual for the poetry of the psalms) but a *formula of faith.*

The relationship between God and the individual that is normally expressed in affective terms is presented more clinically and objectively in Ps 136.

> O give thanks to the Lord, for he is good,
> for his steadfast love endures for ever.
> O give thanks to the God of gods,
> for his steadfast love endures for ever.
> O give thanks to the Lord of lords,
> for his steadfast love endures for ever.
> (vv. 1–3)

Here the God who is encountered and liturgically acclaimed is a God of 'love' — that is, he is seen by the believing community as one who manifests something that is identifiable in human terms with 'steadfast love'. It is clearly *not* an abstraction for the psalmist. It is a reality experienced in history, and as such it determines the response of the worshipper. The translation is in fact deceptive: the word in Hebrew can mean many things — 'love', or 'faith' or 'trust'; it is as complex as human relationships normally are. And because of that, the psalm sets out to strip layer after layer from the idea. After the initial ritual exhortation to give thanks, it presents first Creation (vv. 4–9) and then Redemption (vv. 10–22) as divine interventions made in the reader's history for his benefit:

> to him who by understanding made the heavens,
>   for his steadfast love endures for ever;
> to him who spread out the earth upon the waters,
>   for his steadfast love endures for ever;
> to him who made the great lights,
>   for his steadfast love endures for ever.
>
> to him who smote the first-born of Egypt,
>   for his steadfast love endures for ever;
> and brought Israel out from among them,
>   for his steadfast love endures for ever.
>
> (vv. 5–7; 10–11)

On precisely *this* basis follows the call for a response (vv. 23–26) which will acknowledge the *fact* of encounter in a theological manner, by recognizing both Creation and Redemption as acts of unmerited 'love':

> It is he who remembered us in our low estate,
>   for his steadfast love endures for ever;
> and rescued us from our foes,
>   for his steadfast love endures for ever;
> he who gives food to all flesh,
>   for his steadfast love endures for ever.
>
> O give thanks to the God of heaven,
>   for his steadfast love endures for ever.
>
> (vv. 23–26)

The refrain, 'his steadfast love endures forever', becomes a declaration of *faith* in something specific, and vv. 23–26 become a theological explanation. God's love is not perceived as metaphor for grace, but as a complex of real interventions on the psalmist's account:

> God made the heavens — that was an act of 'love'; he made the sun and moon to give *me* light — that is 'love'; and he brought *me* out from Egyptian bondage — indeed, an act of love.

The psalm is not dealing with an abstraction called 'love' but with a real, historical act of personal regard. The choral acknowledgement — that is, 'endures forever' — emphasizes the present actuality of the divine gift and is clearly a formula that expresses the way Israel understood God and understood religion. Faith is a response to a complex reality that may be explored step by step and so apprehended experientially. As each limited experience is assimilated it goes to make up one cumulative experience of God's action in an individual's history that equals 'love'.

Possibly more than any other psalm, Ps 136 shows that to biblical man 'faith' is neither a *belief in* something nor an 'acceptance of the unseen', but a form of *knowledge* based on experience. This comes across in the responsorial nature of the psalm, where the second half of each verse is a congregational response to a leader's (priest or levite?) statement of fact presented in the first half. It is noteworthy that the 'act of faith' in each case is a statement of God's 'love', and (given the nature of poetic parallelism) that means that the first half defines the concept. Thus 'love', which might otherwise remain a philosophical abstraction, becomes instead a concrete attitude of God towards man — real and experimentable; and 'faith' becomes an equally concrete attitude of man to God in acknowledgement.

In Ps 89 'love' and 'faith' combine in a quasi-formal refrain that dominates the prayer (vv. 2, 5, 8, 14, 24, 33 and 49) and effectively determines the human attitude to God. The act of faith is presented in vv. 1–4:

> I will sing of thy steadfast love, O Lord, for ever;
> with my mouth I will proclaim thy faithfulness to all generations.
> For thy steadfast love was established for ever,
> thy faithfulness is firm as the heavens.
> Thou hast said, 'I have made a covenant with my chosen one,
> I have sworn to David my servant:
> "I will establish your descendants for ever,
> and build your throne for all generations".'

The two terms, 'love' and 'faithfulness', are developed in the rest of the psalm within the context of the community's own experience, where in fact the divine promise to Abraham *was* fulfilled in the Davidic dynasty (vv. 20–38), and so God the creator has shown himself to *be* reliable. The basis of the psalmist's attitude of faith is thus the historical reality of the covenant made with David, and on this is founded his prayer for a continuation of this 'love' (vv. 19ff) in times of personal tribulation (vv. 38ff). He *has* kept his promise to Abraham — he *will therefore* be faithful to the individual in *his* need:

> But now thou hast cast off and rejected,
> thou art full of wrath against thy anointed.
> Thou hast renounced the covenant with thy servant.
> (vv. 38–39a)

The fact that the disaster in question cannot clearly be determined may suggest that in *any* time of need the national confidence can rest on an indisputable fact of history. Furthermore, the opening verses of this psalm have made it clear that faith is passed on from one generation to another by means of the personal witness of individuals who themselves (directly or indirectly) have experienced God's faithfulness and love. Both concepts are inseparable when the fulness of divine act and human response is being explored, for just as the original divine attitude was complex, so is the consequent human one. For this reason, 'steadfast love' and 'fidelity' are almost always paired in those psalms that set out to communicate the *content* of the experience of God. They were not abstractions to the Hebrew mind, but concrete attitudes; and more — attitudes that were determined by the actual situation of the psalmist and the content of the experience to which he responded.

In various psalms one finds attitudes that respond to existential situations — 'faith' for Ps 95 has a significance that is clearly individuated and limited. In the 'credal' formulations, however, these become more universal, have developed into expressions of a sophisticated theology; and so individual words such as 'love', 'faith', 'trust' take on a deeper significance; become less subjective, more clinical and objective. This sets up a chain reaction. The primary attitude of faith is one that is determined for each individual by his apperception of the divine intervention, and each such act of faith and love then becomes a testimony to others of what God has done in a concrete situation. The cycle of experience-response is continually renewed.

Psalm 135 is a very comprehensive *credo*, presenting, in one panoramic sweep, the totality of Israel's experience of God. Verses 5–12 recapitulate Creation, Exodus, the Wilderness experience and the first historical fulfilment of the divine promise:

> He it is who makes the clouds rise at the end of the earth,
> who makes lightnings for the rain
> and brings forth the wind from his storehouses.
>
> He it was who smote the first-born of Egypt,
> both of man and of beast;
> who in thy midst, O Egypt, sent signs and wonders
> against Pharaoh and all his servants;
> who smote many nations and slew mighty kings,
> Sihon, king of the Amorites, and Og, king of Bashan, and all the kingdoms of Canaan,
> and gave their lands as a heritage, a heritage to his people Israel.
> (vv. 7–12)

In other words, the whole credal content of the Old Testament, summed up in two great themes of Creation and Redemption, is presented to the individual for his assent of faith. This experience of the divine activity is made actual by a formal, hymn-type ritual in vv. 13–14:

> Thy name, O Lord, endures for ever,
> thy renown, O Lord, throughout all ages.
> For the Lord will vindicate his people,
> and have compassion on his servants

and this calls for a concrete double-response that represents 'faith': a negative response, the rejection of religious compromise in vv. 15–18, and a positive one, acclamation and praise in vv. 19–21. The reaction to the totality of the divine gift that this psalm represents is both comprehensive and firmly apprehended on the empirical level, as is seen in v. 5:

> For *I know* that the Lord is great,
> and that our Lord is above all gods.

The Hebrew text is more apodictic, as the verb 'to know' maintains its usual connotation of experiential knowledge. This marks the human response represented later by vv. 15–21 as both individual and concrete.

The Implications of Faith

The picture of religious faith that one gets in the psalms is very sapiential, in the sense that the psalmist's concept of God and consequent response to him is based throughout on historical experience. The title of the psalter in the Hebrew bible is 'Praises', but the word preserves overtones of 'recognition' and 'acceptance', always with reference to a datum of experience, be that an actual event or a promise that has been redeemed.

Psalm 25 is a case in point. The introductory statement sets the tone for what follows:

> To thee, O Lord, I lift up my soul.
> O my God, in thee I trust,
>   let me not be put to shame;
>   let not my enemies exult over me.
> Yea, let none that wait for thee be put to shame;
>   let them be ashamed who are wantonly treacherous.
> (vv. 1–3)

Only God can really be 'trusted' — the word signifying a subjective confidence based on historical fact: he *has* proved true, for I have found it so! For this very reason, living a 'life of faith' becomes a concrete, personal response to a *known* God:

> Make me to know thy ways, O Lord; teach me thy paths.
> Lead me in thy truth, and teach me,
>   for thou art the God of my salvation;
>   for thee I wait all the day long.
> Be mindful of thy mercy, O Lord, and of thy steadfast love,
>   for they have been from of old.
> (vv. 4–6)

The poet has learned what Yahweh is like from personal experience of his 'love and mercy' (v. 6), thus making it clear that his faith is a response to a grace of forgiveness, once given and perennially valid (v. 8). There is an interesting theological development latent under the verbal skin: a more or less *emotional* attitude (v. 2: 'trust') hardening into an intellectual conviction (v. 6: God's 'steadfast love . . . has been from of old') and both culminating in an empirical faith (v. 10: 'all the paths of the Lord are steadfast love and faithfulness, for those who keep his covenant . . .'). The initial act of confidence was founded on experience of God's acts of kindness in the past (v. 5), and these are a constant for him (v. 6b). 'Trust' becomes, in its articulation, a human reliance on grace as the psalmist recalls his own failure in fidelity (v. 7).

In fact, the whole of this psalm sees 'love' in terms of a divine grace, for while the Covenant is a guarantee of Yahweh's fidelity the author is aware of the fact that his own actual betrayal (vv. 7, 8 and 11) has relieved God of any forensic obligation he might have had. As a result the reaction of faith that he presents is closer to gratitude and dependence than to abstract 'belief'. This theology of forgiveness is buttressed by knowledge of the fact that the Covenant had originally established man in a special relationship to God for no other reason than a gratuitous urge of divine love. The psalmist's recognition of this fact has a strange result. In the second part of the psalm, from v. 11 onward, it is as if this love of God's for a faithless covenant-partner becomes a source of healing for the psalmist. And the mutual relationship of 'love and fidelity' that marked the spring-time of covenant-faith is renewed:

> Who is the man that fears the Lord?
> Him will he instruct in the way that he should choose.
> He himself shall abide in prosperity,
> and his children shall possess the land.
> The friendship of the Lord is for those who fear him,
> and he makes known to them his covenant.
> My eyes are ever toward the Lord,
> for he will pluck my feet out of the net.
> (vv. 12–15)

Quite clearly, this has marked implications for theology. The practice of religion is seen to be a *relationship*, initiated by God and maintained by him, rather than something achieved by man. It is the act of an individual who chooses to stand in a right relationship to God *within a context already determined by God*. He sees man in all his humanity, sows in him the seed of desire, and himself cultivates the resultant growth. Receptivity is all that is required on man's part.

Psalm 40 explains a lot about this relationship. Its structure is immediately strange to the eye — contrary to the usual 'Lament-form', the prayer of thanksgiving *precedes* the request for aid in time of personal need, thus reversing the progress of lament. This surely points to the fact that as a psalm it represents a declaration of faith rather than a petition. That is to say, the cry for help when it does come (in vv. 11–17) is motivated by concrete experience of God's intervention in the past, and it is precisely this that fuels the appeal to God's fidelity and loving grace in v. 11b (where the composite formula for 'faith' is used). The inner tension evident in Ps 40 indicates the theological nature of this faith rather than the personal. The first section, vv. 1–10, reflects the psalmist's gratitude for a *known and experienced* act of deliverance:

> He inclined to me and heard my cry.
> He drew me up from the desolate pit,
> out of the miry bog.
>
> (vv. 1b–2)

while vv. 11–17 is a prayer in time of distress. This prayer is tied to the faith of the psalmist. That is, it is a subjective reaction to an objective experience. 'Love' and 'faithfulness' in v. 11 are thus defined in terms of God's past, historical intervention.

In the opening affirmation of vv. 1–3 the emphasis is on God and what he has done, rather than on the actual need of the psalmist — which remains symbolic, a dramatization of alienation. This is in sharp contrast to vv. 11–12 where the emphasis is very clearly on the personal plight of the poet. An interesting note is introduced by the 'new song' motif in v. 3. It is thought necessary to prescind from a 'traditional' form of psalmody, perhaps, because the experience of distress is personal and thus an equally personal expression seems called for. The same phrase is found in two other psalms (33,3 and 144,9) where God has shown himself to be trustworthy. Very clearly in Ps 40 the 'faith' of the psalmist (see vv. 4 and 6) is based on God's love for him; a manifestation of grace in the past which evokes a precise attitude of 'trust' from both the psalmist himself and those of his community who have witnessed this exercise of divine love. This historical love is further defined in vv. 12–14, and serves as a continuing source of faith in the recurrent difficulties of vv. 15–16.

The Development of Faith

Thus experience of a divine act in one's favour may lead to an attitude of prayer that can be described as 'faith' — yet this faith does not spring up full-grown and mature in the life of Israel. It must be continually cultivated, continually built-up by re-evocation of the faith-object (experience) of the past. And this tension of 'begun but not yet perfected' is apparent throughout the whole of the second part of Ps 40. In a way, the first part exhibited the grounds of faith, while this second part exhibits a human attitude that is a blend of faith and hope. This is particularly true of vv. 13–16:

> Be pleased, O Lord, to deliver me!
>   O Lord, make haste to help me!
> Let them be put to shame and confusion altogether
>   who seek to snatch away my life;
> let them be turned back and brought to dishonour
>   who desire my hurt!
> Let them be appalled because of their shame
>   who say to me, 'Aha, Aha!'
> But may all who seek thee
>   rejoice and be glad in thee;
> may those who love thy salvation
>   say continually, 'Great is the Lord!'

Prayer is both the expression of this faith-hope attitude and the force that sustains and grounds hope. This idea of 'workaday faith' is psychologically perceptive: a combination of firm belief and hopeful expectation, the whole tinged with a natural human anxiety (v. 12 leading to the formal prayer of vv. 13ff).

Verses 6–8 represent a disposition that is known as 'faith and love' *on man's part* — his reaction to God. And it is remarkably interiorized: reminiscent of the 'entrance liturgies', it is ethical rather than ritual. It culminates in a powerful statement of personal intimacy: 'I *delight* in the expression of your personality, Lord', where the word 'delight' is one frequently used in sexual contexts. The meaning, perhaps, is that of total surrender of the self to God and absorption in him. This profound faith now endows the poet with the capacity to become, himself, an 'object' of faith-encounter for others; in him God's 'faithful love' becomes present to, and open to being experienced by, others.

> I have not hid thy saving help within my heart;
>   I have spoken of thy faithfulness and thy salvation;
>   I have not concealed thy steadfast love and thy faithfulness
>   from the great congregation.
>
> (v. 10)

Thus Ps 40 may stand as the classic statement of faith in the psalter, with vv. 1–3a representing the faith-experience (divine intervention); vv. 4–8 the human reaction (faith as an attitude of response); and

vv. 9–10 the psalmist as sacrament of encounter (the object of second-generation faith).

Something of the same kind is reflected in Ps 115,1–3, where the poet's concern is that God's love and fidelity should be effective realities in the world of the here and now, that this should be evident to all, and thereby influence the faith of everyone. In all probability this psalm was originally antiphonal, so that a presentation of divine reality is answered by a declaration of faith *that is evoked by that presentation.* This is especially clear in vv. 9–11 which present the living God, as the experiences of previous generations (Creation, and perhaps Covenant) are actualized in the cult and are matched by a congregational response (vv. 12–13). The God who *has* created all *is still* involved in Israel's life.

In the later tradition — that of the pluralist society of post-exilic Israel — 'faith' takes on a more secular colouring. One example of this is Ps 37, a very disorganized poem consisting of scattered topics rather than any one unified theme. Whatever unity exists is provided by the motif 'trust', a word that normally signals a later development in Israel's understanding of faith. The word itself occurs in v. 3 and v. 5, while various images of trust occur in v. 7f, v. 18 and v. 21. Effectively, the psalm is a collection of wisdom proverbs. This means that the 'object' presented for the reader's response is not directly a divine intervention; rather, a series of word-pictures, each one based on some aspect of human experience, is placed before the reader — possession of the land (v. 3ff), the natural law of act-consequence (vv. 7ff, 14f, 16), social experience (v. 18f). Being a wisdom psalm, the motivation for response is personal, secular experience. Thus the reader's capacity to say to each situation so presented 'yes, I have found it so' fixes a state of mind that may be summed up in the concept 'trust' — the more human face of religion.

For the author of Ps 37 faith is an active virtue. Verses 7–8 even describe it in terms of simple character-training:

> Be still before the Lord, and wait patiently for him;
> fret not yourself over him who prospers in his way,
> over the man who carries out evil devices!
> Refrain from anger, and forsake wrath!
> Fret not yourself; it tends only to evil;

forming the habit of attending to experience and finding there the voice of God filtered through the logic of existence. Trust of this kind does not come naturally—one must learn it the hard way, train oneself to listen. This positive attitude of confidence in God is the logical corollary to the common-sense principle that if God exists he must surely be in control. And since the cosmic order and the laws of nature testify to this the natural reaction is reliance on the divinity for success in life. There is an interior logic to faith: every human act carries within itself the seed of its own implications (vv. 14–15). Thus one's own human attitude can elicit a response from God (vv. 18–20), can set up a chain-reaction as that divine grace draws from man the urge to share its fruits with others (vv. 21–22).

Psalm 37 thus represents a later, sapiential development of the concept 'faith', as v. 25 with its wisdom ethos attests:

> I have been young, and now am old;
> yet I have not seen the righteous forsaken
> or his children begging bread.

Common human experience, rather than theologically interpreted divine intervention, becomes the 'object' that provokes a reaction, that forms an attitude which is seen as 'trust' rather than 'faith' in the more theological sense; everyday holiness rather than covenant religion. The daily grind of 'just carrying on with life' is sustained by a rational confidence in the created order that is more at home in the kitchen than in the cult.

CHAPTER 3

A WITNESSING COMMUNITY

There is a prescription in the Law of Moses that indicates the true meaning of 'community' for Israel: 'three times a year shall you appear before the Lord God' (Ex 23,17). This is an injunction laid upon the twelve-tribe confederacy to go up each year to the tribal sanctuary to worship, for it was pre-eminently in this act that 'Israel' found and expressed its identity in the face of an alien world. The three occasions referred to were the feasts of Passover, Weeks (or Pentecost) and Tabernacles (or variously 'booths', 'huts', 'tents'), all historical celebrations that memorialized the major events of salvation-history.

Passover recalled the Exodus, Weeks the Sinai experience and Tabernacles the crossing of the desert. The psalms that were chanted during these festivals were mainly those that recalled the great, creative moments of the past, and they were recited in the sanctuary so that they might evoke once more the acts done by God long ago that made them his people. Thus they all contain an element of catechesis. The history and tradition of a people is passed on — not as a dead letter but as a living element still at work in the present day. Remembrance of Exodus, the Covenant and the wilderness wandering plays a large part in these psalms because of their primary theological function of re-evocation or 'sacramentality'.

In evoking the past event of Exodus Israel was reminded of the redemption that was hers by inheritance, and of the eschatological fulfilment for which they hoped — the *shalom* that was the breath of their theological existence. For later ages — aliens on a foreign shore — this expectation took on a brooding note of longing: 'by the waters of Babylon, there we sat down and wept when we remembered Zion . . . let my tongue cleave to the roof of my mouth . . . if I do not set Jerusalem above my highest joy!' (Ps 137).

Weeks placed before them the moment of challenge, the covenant with God by which they became his 'special people' and in which they assumed the obligations that are endemic to so exclusive a religion.

Tabernacles, or the celebration of the Wilderness, presented a compound image, at once a joyful memory of the springtime of faith that the desert always suggested and a reminder of the compromise that lay at the heart of their existence 'among the nations' in the land they had occupied. A nation set apart to God can never be less than a nation that gives exclusive witness.

The Meaning of Election

The psalms that reflect this cultic observance were intended to insert contemporary Israel into its historical and theological past by teaching each new generation how to take hold of its origins and thus respond for itself before the God who had marked them as his own.

Psalm 95 is perhaps the most representative of these, and like its companions can best be described as a psalm of 'personal commitment' and awareness of vocation. Each member of God's people is given a chance to make a new start — first in *knowledge*, then in *piety*, and thus to renew at its source the response that *is* 'faith'. Quite simply, Ps 95 presents God to his people as Creator and Redeemer, reminds them of the implications of election, and compels them to act accordingly. In this way the double event of creation-covenant is renewed in the life of Israel — but this time less as a creed than as an outright challenge. Already that much can be inferred from the introduction in vv. 1–2, where the divine title 'rock of our salvation' determines the nature of the response. In this designation the past (Ex 17) and its eschatological fulfilment combine in one moment of crisis, as God makes himself present to the people gathered before him in the cult. The *immediate* implications appear in vv. 3–5:

> For the Lord is a great God,
>   and a great King above all gods.
> In his hand are the depths of the earth;
>   the heights of the mountains are his also.
> The sea is his, for he made it;
>   for his hands formed the dry land.

While this is a theologoumenon — 'the heights of the mountains are his' being an affirmation of the totality of Yahweh's dominion over his creatures — it is in fact no more than a preliminary step in the total thrust of the psalm. The affirmation that God is *universal* creator determines that acclamation in v. 6 which represents the natural response of *all* peoples to the divinity.

> O come, let us worship and bow down,
> let us kneel before the Lord, our *maker*.

This can be said by every theist.

But this is now expanded by the introduction of a new motive — the covenant formula poetically re-phrased in vv. 7a–c.

> For he is *our* God,
> and *we* are the people of his pasture,
> and the sheep of his hand.

This can only be said by Israel, and so the very structure of the psalm makes its point: a general confession that *all* creatures are dependent on God and must respond appropriately serves to highlight the more particular relationship that exists *for Israel* as a result of the Sinai experience, and thus emphasizes the essentially different response demanded of them. Israel's covenant relationship to God calls for much more than the common response of the acknowledged creature. He is more than their creator; with them he made an alliance, calling them to a special intimacy. Here in v. 7c the formula of the covenant shows the motive for Israel's response, for it embodies their understanding of the Sinai experience. Alliance, or covenant, was seen to be less a bipartite relationship than a commissioning to service. God chooses a people to collaborate with him in achieving his purpose. Theologically, then, a covenant relationship is a call to service that places man at the disposition of the God who selects him. Thus the Sinai experience means more than simple election or protection — it implies a common task to be achieved. And it is this divine intention that gives it its theological meaning. The Covenant remains essentially a divine project.

This, then, is recapitulated and presented anew in Ps 95. Verse 7d stresses the reality of it all — the 'today' of recitation is as real a moment of crisis as Meribah and Massah had been to an earlier generation:

> O that *today* you would hearken to his voice!
> harden not your hearts . . .
> as your fathers did *on that day* at Massah.

Two 'days' of decision are contraposed. The psalm speaks of a sacramental encounter in which Israel meets the God who not only created but called her from among all other nations to an exclusive service.

The theological structure of these seven verses is suggestive. The coming together of the two themes — creation and covenant — is relatively unusual for the Old Testament. It belongs properly to the late period, after the Exile, when Deutero-Isaiah used the joint concept of Yahweh as Creator-Redeemer — the universal creator-God who will re-create the world lost by sin in a new 'Exodus' that will re-establish the covenant. Is 43, 8–21 in fact ends with a new gift of water in the desert, reminiscent of Ex 17,6 and the life-giving 'rock' that is the opening symbolism of the psalm. Ps 95, like Is 43, recovers a note of obligation inherent in the covenant relationship.

Israel had been chosen for a double divine purpose: to be, by her existence in history, a witness to Yahweh's redemptive intention; and thus to testify to his nature as *one* God and universal creator. Her role was therefore not a passive one — to become holy; but one that involved certain responsibility for the salvation of others. This had been laid down by the call of Abraham in Gen 12, prototype of all vocation within the covenant people. This responsibility was that of paying exclusive worship to God by a manner of life that was, though restrictive in human terms, spiritually liberating; and thus to exercise a positive role in the divine salvific plan of mediating blessing 'to all the families of the earth' (Gen 12,3).

These are the implications of the Sinai experience that is now presented in Ps 95,1–7c, and the reader is prepared for the challenge that follows in vv. 7d–11:

> O that today you would hearken to his voice!
> Harden not your hearts, as at Meribah,
> as on the day at Massah in the wilderness,
> when your fathers tested me,
> and put me to the proof, though they had seen my work.
> For forty years I loathed that generation
> and said, 'they are a people who err in heart,
> and they do not regard my ways'.
> Therefore I swore in my anger
> that they should not enter my rest.

The community that has gathered to recite this psalm is thereby called to make the same personal decision regarding their lives that

Sinai itself had demanded of Moses and his followers — '*today*, therefore, listen to his voice, and do not harden your hearts . . . '. So vital to the nature of the community is the challenge that after Moses' death Joshua renewed it for the 'new' people gathered around him on the threshold of the promised land (Josh 24,14), almost as a condition of their inheriting the divine promise. This represents the abiding nature of the challenge that being a 'people set apart to God' involves. And it underlines the personal nature of faith. The decision that is to be made is a very individual one, for one cannot inherit the religion of one's forefathers, and their commitment cannot bind their successors. In each case the decision is made on the basis of the reality experienced, either historically at Sinai or sacramentally 'today' (see Deut 30).

Perhaps Ps 95 can best be seen as a re-statement of Gen 12 and the theology of vocation. There, out of all mankind impotent under sin, one people was chosen to be special collaborators in, and servants of, the divine purpose of redemption:

> Now the Lord said to Abram . . . I will make of you a
> great nation, and I will bless you, and make your
> name great, so that you will be a blessing . . . and by
> you all the families of the earth will receive
> blessing. (Gen 12,1–3)

This results in an élite vocation and a consequent, exclusive, way of life that is the 'sacrament' of the divine intention (see Deut 7,6ff). Ps 95 gives an edge of actuality to this.

Psalm 81 expands the basic idea by noting how the exclusive nature of covenant religion demands a particular level of dedication to God — that which in fact *constituted* Israel. As has been observed, the opening verses are clearly meant to be a sacramental actualization of redemption. The liturgical oracle that follows in v. 5c prepares the reader for a special divine 'word':

> I heard a voice I had not known:

The voice is that of Yahweh himself, and the half-verse is the turning point of the psalm. It presents the Exodus-event as an experience in the reader's 'today', and places before him very clearly the consequent, fundamental exigence of the relationship so forged:

I relieved *your* shoulder of the burden;
 your hands were freed from the basket.
In distress *you* called, and I delivered *you*;
 I answered *you* in the secret place of thunder;
 I tested *you* at the waters of Meribah.
Hear, O my people, while I admonish you!
 O Israel, if you would but listen to me!
There shall be no strange god among you;
 you shall not bow down to a foreign god.

The last verse, with all its implications, is a summary of Israel's religion. Just as failure to observe this leads to the annihilation of the community, so observance of what the covenant demands establishes the community in its redemptive role (vv. 13–16).

The service of God is perceived less as obligation than as joyful giving; vocation is the start of a journey into freedom.

The Vocation of the Community

How, or what, does this call to 'be holy to Yahweh' contribute to the divine purpose of salvation?

Israel's existence as an identifiable community rested on a double theological principle: past salvation and present history converge for each generation; so also does salvation-history and vocation. An example of this is found in the way Ps 114 views the community vocation of witness:

When Israel went forth from Egypt,
 the house of Jacob from a people of strange language,
Judah became his sanctuary,
 Israel his dominion.
The sea looked and fled,
 Jordan turned back.
The mountains skipped like rams,
 the hills like lambs.
 (vv. 1–4)

The events of Exodus depicted here are considered to be events that have an actual value for the contemporary community, and this generates an inner tension between the creation of the community at Exodus (vv. 1–4) and its present function in the contemporary world (vv. 7–8). The interrogative structure of the intervening section, vv. 5–6, effectively links the Red Sea theophany of the opening verses with the presence of God effected by Israel's existence in history:

What ails you, O sea, that you flee?
O Jordan, that you turn back?
O mountains, that you skip like rams?
O hills, like lambs?

(vv. 5–6)

The Psalmist's interrogation of mute creation — using the continuous form of the verb: 'why *are you* fleeing, sea; why *are you now* turning back, Jordan? . . .' — underlines the contemporaneity of the Exodus-event. God is present to the sea *now* as he was *then* because Israel is present to the situation. In fact, the question is deliberately provocative: 'what ails you, O sea?' (v. 5) follows on the historical statement that 'the sea looked, and fled' (v. 3). Israel must *think*, and recognize its own role!

Of much greater importance in establishing the nature of the worshipping community is Ps 105, a recapitulation of the history of salvation from the call of Abraham (Gen 12) to the present day of the poet; an unfolding drama of God's relationship to his people up to their ('our') entry into the promised land. These are the events that forged the nation's identity and are therefore essential to her self-knowledge and her knowledge of God. The psalm is a formal credal statement, and it is therefore a classic piece of catechesis — introducing a new generation to that commitment that constitutes faith. It is quite a late composition, presenting a modern, and theologically sophisticated view of religion. Several things about it warn the reader to take a look behind the scenes and understand its latent force. In itself, the first part (vv. 1–6) makes it clear that it is technically a liturgical act, and vv. 9–10 speak of handing on the covenant commitment from one generation to another. Furthermore, the whole poem is woven into the liturgical setting of 1 Chron 16, a text that deals with the establishment of Sion as the theological focus of the nation's unity. So it is immediately clear to the reader that he is dealing with the familiar principle of sacramental re-presentation of a saving event by means of recital.

As an introduction to the sacramental 'word' that will follow, vv. 1–6 summon the reader (that is, 'the offspring of Abraham' of v. 6) to re-experience for himself those 'wonderful works' of redemption that God performed for his ancestors (v. 5), *with a view to 'making these known' to all peoples* (v. 1):

O give thanks to the Lord, call on his name,
  make known his deeds among the peoples!
Sing to him, sing praises to him,
  tell of all his wonderful works!
Glory in his holy name;
  let the hearts of those who seek the Lord rejoice!
Seek the Lord and his strength,
  seek his presence continually!
Remember the wonderful works that he has done,
  his miracles, and the judgments he uttered,
O offspring of Abraham his servant,
  sons of Jacob, his chosen ones!

On the basis of this 'now' experience, the pious Israelite *himself* becomes for others the sacrament of that primal experience of redemption. Verse 7ff now shows how this is worked out in practice, as (following the traditional form of 'recital') the worshipper responds to the self-revelation of the saving God that has just taken place by means of the liturgical re-presentation of the divine event. This human response is, first of all, a renewal of personal awareness of covenant, and then an acceptance of its implications. And it shows the particular perspective that governed the life of each Israelite — how the community interpreted its own history as a continuation of Yahweh's acts throughout time; acts that served as stimuli to lead men to salvation; acts that they could re-experience as present realities related to their own lives. The annihilation of the difference between past and present is evident in vv. 7–11:

He is the Lord our God;
  his judgments are in all the earth.
He is mindful of his covenant for ever,
  of the word that he commanded, for a thousand generations.
the covenant which he made with Abraham,
  his sworn promise to Isaac,
which he confirmed to Jacob as a statute,
  to Israel as an everlasting covenant,
saying, 'To you I will give the land of Canaan
  as your portion for an inheritance.'

From this point on the rest of the drama unfolds scene by scene: the Wilderness experience (vv. 12–15), the story of Joseph (vv. 16–25), the Exodus itself (fittingly treated in detail. vv. 26–41). Finally, the extinction of the first generation, which alone had enjoyed first-hand experience of Exodus (vv. 42–44), brings the reader full-circle: back to his own second-generation situation of one who never saw the historical Sinai. Yet he is abundantly aware that he has *in fact* experienced the saving reality of Sinai sacramentally, so now he can break into a paean of joy and praise:

> And he gave them (us) the lands of the nations;
> and they took possession of the fruit of other peoples' toil,
> to the end that they should keep his statutes,
> and observe his laws.
> Praise the Lord!
> (vv. 44–45)

It is precisely here, in v. 45, that awareness dawns; that one realizes how covenant vocation involves covenant responsibility, as divine grace evokes human response:

> keep his statutes!
> observe his law!
> praise the Lord!

The Testimony of Praise

The Old Testament is the expression in words of what God meant to Israel — and so the whole of her life *as* a people was meant to be a fitting response.

Thus praise is the most characteristic mode of existence for the community, and the most human of attitudes. In Hebrew the psalter is entitled 'Praises', and the spirit is summed-up in the way Ps 22,3 sees the relationship between Israel and her God, who is 'enthroned on the praises of Israel'. Indeed, the activity of praising Yahweh is analogous to life itself, as is clear from the many psalms in which the inability to do so is likened to death (such as Pss 6; 13; 88). The reality of God embraces all space and time; a reality that may be encountered at any level of life, for God is so much part of the human ambient that to exist is to be in his presence.

Psalm 36 recognizes the sweeping reality of this fact:

> Thy righteousness is like the mountains of God,
> thy judgements are like the great deep;
> man and beast thou savest, O Lord.
> (v. 6)

Even the beasts are part of the reality that God embraces. By recalling this fact the psalmist seeks to evoke the greatness, fidelity and justice of Yahweh, so as to lead the reader to dialogue (v. 7):

> How precious is thy steadfast love, O God!
> The children of men take refuge in the shadow of thy wings.

The central perception — that God is the focus of existence, the ultimate reality that embraces all living things — leads to the realization that fulness of life can only mean life lived in communion with God; life lived as a testimony *to* God. Without him, man is what the earth becomes without water; with him, existence itself is a garden of delight (vv. 8–9):

> They feast on tthe abundance of thy house,
> and thou givest them drink from the river of thy delights.
> For with thee is the fountain of life;
> in thy light do we see light.

These verses underline the quality of life with God. By initiating an act of praise the Israelite enters into a communion with the Creator that overflows into the lives of all those with whom he shares his experience. He becomes a channel of the 'steadfast love' of God for others of the community (v. 10). Now, after his experience of God's intervention, the believer can begin to make sense of the world of 'the other' that encroaches upon him — a world that God seeks, in which he can be experienced and through which humanity assumes its real value. Thus man reflects the 'glory of Yahweh' in his world and in so doing becomes fully a person.

The sacramental role of Israel as a witnessing community becomes more explicit in Ps 47, where the divine interventions of salvation-history are presented as ever-living realities borne on the stream of Israel's existence among the nations, where they become contemporary events in the lives of all. Whatever specific liturgy these verses were originally meant to accompany — the entrance of the Ark of the Covenant into the Temple, perhaps, or the Enthronement of Yahweh as king — the 'saving' aspect of the divine governance is repeated throughout history, and by recitation given a present salvific value for all — Jew and Gentile alike (see vv. 3, 4 and 7).

The psalm begins with an invitation that consists of a double-imperative in v. 1:

> Clap your hands, all peoples!
> Shout to God with loud songs of joy!

The motivational clause that duly follows removes all doubt that God's kingship is eternal, and that his *universal* reign is the scope of all his historical acts of redemption — acts that are now at work in the present (vv. 2–4):

For the Lord, the Most High, is terrible,
a great king over all the earth.
He subdued peoples under us,
and nations under our feet.
He chose our heritage for us,
the pride of Jacob whom he loves.

Those who are celebrating clearly represent all the peoples of the world — and the purpose of their acclamation is that all, and not just Israel, may come to recognize Yahweh as ruler. The motivation is Gods' *fearful* majesty, and fear of God is characteristic of *all* peoples. The formulation of vv. 3–4 is clumsy in Hebrew — God 'subdues peoples under' Israel and 'choosing our heritage' — and runs limpingly at best. This suggests an artificial structure that is meant to draw universal implications from the exclusive covenant relationship of 'God and his special people'. It is a universal extension of that relationship, mediated by the children 'of Jacob whom he loves'. The faith of Israel is rooted in the divine activity in history, in acts that demonstrated both his greatness and his will to save. The recitation of this psalm becomes a moment in time when that specific, past grace becomes a present reality. As a result, the distance between heaven and earth is destroyed and, as it were, the scene on earth is placed side by side with the heavenly reality of Yahweh's universal rule. This is brought out by the use of the present, continuous tense in vv. 8–9:

God reigns over the nations;
God sits on his holy throne.
The princes of the peoples gather
as the people of the God of Abraham.
For the shields of the earth belong to God;
he is highly exalted!

Saving history has come full-circle from the promise to Abraham in Gen 12 that '. . . in you all the nations will (in the future) be blessed', to the present situation of the singer, '. . . the people gather (now) as the people of the God of Abraham' (v. 9b).

It is precisely this tension between 'then' and 'now', 'Israel' and 'the nations', that unifies Ps 47. The introductory imperative of v. 1, 'clap your hands, *all* peoples', immediately raises the question: why should *they,* and not only his *own* people, praise the God of Israel? The answer is found in the universal nature of his supremacy, and this is stated in apodictic terms in vv. 2–4. The logic of language forces the conclusion that this is the present state of the 'nations' (vv. 7–9). What, therefore, has happened to bring this about? It can only be Israel's psalmic recitation in praise of the *covenant* God, and indeed this *is* presented as the linking factor in vv. 5–6 with its burden, 'sing praises to God, sing praises! Sing praises to *our* King, sing praises!' So Yahweh's intervention in favour of 'Jacob' must have universal implications that are mediated by the covenant-people's *witness of praise*, which first brings them into the ambient of grace ('subdues peoples under *us*') and then makes it possible for them to share with 'all peoples' on an equal footing the covenant relationship to a common King ('the princes of the people gathering just as the people of the God of Abraham'). The strict parallelism of v. 9ab reinforces the idea that acceptance of the universal nature of God's kingdom precipitates acceptance on the part of the 'new Israel', and gathers in the nations. The dimension of 'praise' found in Ps 47 is a theological perception of vocation: recognition of Yahweh's lordship of history means recognition of the fact that history has a wider potential than the vindication of Israel *before* the nations. God's history evolves towards the vindication of *all* the peoples of the earth, and Israel stands within that history *as mediator of that process.*

This is the function of God's forgiving and healing love throughout history, as Ps 103 suggests: 'Bless the Lord, O my soul! . . . for he forgives all your iniquity and heals all your diseases'. What is immediately noticeable is the categoric nature of the introductory phrase (vv. 1–2), and the sequence of staccato interjections that follows (vv. 3–5). These are stock phrases for the community tradition, but now used in a new, abrupt way they force the reader to reason for himself and to pose the question, 'why this grace for *me*?'

> Bless the Lord, O my soul;
>   and all that is within me, bless his holy name!
> Bless the Lord, O my soul,
>   and forget not all his benefits,
> who forgives all your iniquity,
>   who heals all your diseases,

who redeems your life from the Pit,
who crowns you with steadfast love and mercy,
who satisfies you with good as long as you live
so that your youth is renewed like the eagle's.
(vv. 1–5)

It is obviously not due to personal merit, for in fact 'he does not deal with us according to our sins, nor requite us according to our iniquities' (v. 10). So why such a demonstration of redemptive concern?

Since the psalm is a parable of God's history of redemption, the answer must be found in its structure, if anywhere. The chiastic arrangement of the psalm brings this out. God's redemptive intervention on behalf of the individual (here the psalmist himself) in vv. 15–18 becomes the hinge of a diptych, or composite picture, the two panels of which are formed by vv. 6–14 and vv. 19–22. Thus:

vv. 6–14: God
His acts of vindication
in Exodus and creation,
and his continuing
'maternal' love in history.

vv. 15–18: Me
Transient and meritless
I have found vindication in
a covenant grace.

vv. 19–22: God
God's kingdom embraces *all*,
and *all* are meant to hear
his word and receive his
grace 'in all places of
his dominion' (v. 22b).

God wishes to involve the *world* in his act of redemption, so he stoops down to the psalmist (and the worshipping community), involves himself in that limited and personal history, and so provokes the process of 'establishing his universal throne in the heavens' (v. 19).

Passing on 'the Faith'

Psalm 78 is a parable of conversion. In it the role of 'witness' is seen from the obverse, the negative side — that of Israel's infidelity to vocation.

Technically it is a historical recital like Ps 105, a recapitulation of the history of salvation that carries the story up to the establishment by David of the city of Sion. That fact, along with the strong wisdom tone adopted by the psalmist, may serve to establish the local and temporal scene: a major festival celebrated before, or immediately after, the break-up of the Davidic dynasty in the tenth century (see 2 Kings 12). It may also explain the atmosphere of guilt that pervades the poem, the mood of disillusion as an older generation broods on its own history of infidelity. What stands out is the catechetical preoccupation of vv. 5–8:

> He established a testimony in Jacob,
> and appointed a law in Israel,
> which he commanded our fathers
> to teach to their children;
> that the next generation might know them,
> the children yet unborn,
> and arise and tell them to their children,
> so that they should set their hope in God,
> and not forget the works of God,
> but keep his commandments;
> and that they should not be like their fathers,
> a stubborn and rebellious generation,
> a generation whose heart was not steadfast,
> whose spirit was not faithful to God.

The psalmist is trying to pass on the fruit of his own experience, his personal knowledge of the implications of Sinai, to a new generation not yet come of age (v. 6), so that they might 'make good' (v. 7) and not repeat the negligence of their forefathers. A keen desire for continuity marks the whole section from v. 2 to v. 8. This naturally determines the didactic tone, the concern to make the implications of religious vocation as real to a prospective third generation as they had been to the first (vv. 42–45), before human respect and a desire to 'belong' among their more sophisticated neighbours in the land of their adoption liberalized the stern realities of the covenant faith. Verses 58–64 describe the period of the conquest of the Promised Land as one of religious compromise, the kind that goes hand-in-hand with political expediency:

For they provoked him to anger with their high places;
they moved him to jealousy with their graven images.
When God heard, he was full of wrath,
and he utterly rejected Israel.
He forsook his dwelling at Shiloh,
the tent where he dwelt among men.

The 'high places' are the sanctuaries of the religion of Canaan, and their mention here reflects the political atmosphere of the times: if one made an alliance with a neighbouring state one accepted their gods into one's own pantheon. It was the normal price of political and social security, and Israel paid it.

The psalm therefore stands as a reminder: first, that central to faith is a covenant between God and his people wherein they accepted certain obligations, one of them being an exclusive service of Yahweh; second, that this constituted an arena of salvation where the human decision of the individual affected the divine salvific plan. Each new generation must know this, with the empirical knowledge of encounter (v. 6) and face up to the implications of vocation. So Ps 78 presents the history of salvation as a parable addressed by God *to the reader*; a creative word that becomes the arena of encounter in which man listens — or, of course, refuses to listen! And the psalmist holds nothing back; he details his own failure and that of his generation with a keen appreciation of human psychology: the first 'no' is easy, almost imperceptible, but once given the individual is swept away on a flood that becomes faster and faster and increasingly difficult to control. It is easy to forget where the line is drawn (v. 11), but if one does then imperceptibly at first one settles in to a compromise that seems logical (vv. 19ff) and ends up a practical apostate (vv. 56ff).

They forgot what he had done,
and the miracles that he had shown them . . .
(So) they tested God in their heart
by demanding the food they craved.
They spoke against God, saying,
'Can God spread a table in the wilderness?
(Certainly) he smote the rock so that water gushed out
and streams overflowed.
(But) can he also give bread,
or provide meat for his people?' . . .
(So) they tested and rebelled against the Most High God,
and did not observe his testimonies,

but turned away and acted
treacherously like their fathers;
they twisted like a deceitful bow.
(vv. 11; 18–20; 56–57)

This parable of 'the apostate's progress' sets off in more dramatic colours the contrast — God's constancy in love/Israel's constant infidelity. This is the theological nucleus, and the term used in the text evokes a divine love that is motherly and vulnerable:

Yet he, being *compassionate*,
forgave their iniquity,
and did not destroy them;
he restrained his anger often,
and did not stir up all his wrath.
He remembered that they were but flesh.
(vv. 38–39a)

The text is an echo of Ex 34. If God allows man to suffer it is only to 'educate' him to the point where he can, like a wilful child, 'come to his senses', respond positively to the offer of forgiveness, and return to his covenant obligations, taking his place in the unfolding of God's saving plan.

In fact, to any clear-headed reader, the great mystery on which the parable is poised is precisely this foolish love of God's — and this forces one to look for the answer within the text of Ps 78 itself. The only solution that is in any way apparent is that God has a plan that is greater than man's infidelity, and that plan must be served by his covenant partner who shares responsibility for re-establishing Sion as the focus of the nations. The prayer of the psalm moves from the great 'miracle of grace' that was Exodus, through the Sinai Covenant, to the founding of Sion and the promise of an eschatological 'Sion' gathered in by a new Davidic shepherd (vv. 68–72):

but he chose the tribe of Judah,
Mount Zion, which he loves.
He built his sanctuary like the high heavens,
like the earth, which he has founded for ever.
He chose David his servant,
and took him from the sheepfolds;
from tending the ewes that had young he brought him
to be shepherd of Jacob his people,
of Israel his inheritance.
With upright heart he tended them,
and guided them with skilful hand.

Psalm 78 stops at this point, abruptly perhaps; but it would be pointless to go further. Enough has been said to make it quite clear that all now depends on Israel's return to an awareness of the implications of religious witness. Thus only Israel can write the rest of the psalm.

CHAPTER 4

THE POETRY OF CREATION

Each individual is born into a material and moral cosmos he did not create and whose origins lie beyond his experience. If a creator exists, he becomes 'real' only by virtue of man's capacity to think. God enters into the human environment only when man brings his intellectual faculties to bear on the known so as to evoke the unknown. Paradoxically enough, 'creation' is a harder concept to grasp than 'redemption'.

The world will always remain a threatening mystery if it cannot be controlled by controlling its point of origin— by arriving at its creator and 'knowing' him. This is essentially a philosophical investigation (though the term would be alien to the Old Testament), and becomes a religious quest only when a personal creator is discovered or postulated. The starting point is usually that sense of the numinous and the contingent that is shared by peoples of diverse race and culture. Israel was no different, but for her that sense of the numinous — which can still be found in the older strata of folk-religion (as Ps 29) — was allied to an experience of historical intervention, and the combination of experience and speculation resulted in a singularly fresh concept of God.

Historically, the theology of 'Creation' is a late-comer on the Old Testament scene, and was due to a felt need to integrate history — that is salvation experienced and expected — with the present situation of Israel among the nations. Effectively, creation as it is found in the Bible is an effort at making religious sense of *what is*, and of explaining the *way it is.* For this reason it serves a practical rather than a philosophical purpose. It gives meaning to a present, known reality — man and his world as they are experienced. For this reason the psalms esteem — by their categories are forced to esteem — the values of the perceptible world. And in this light human life itself is found to have a great potential: it becomes an existence in a known world that is open to improvement because it may be related to a God who has a purpose for it all.

Under the Shadow of Death

The possibility of a divine meaning latent in creation was particularly important for a people whose life was passed under the shadow of death. For the psalter, terrestrial reality was the only one and so death dominated the anthropology of the psalms to a marked degree, even when it was not explicitly invoked. It influenced the way creation was perceived and used. An unsentimental appreciation of mortality brought a clarity of vision to what was perceived as 'the good'. Death was the end of all things human, and this fact tended to focus attention on what was possible, and of value, in earthly terms — as a psalmist with other preoccupations hastens to assert:

> Lord, let me know my end,
> and what is the measure of my days;
> let me know how fleeting my life is!
> Behold, thou hast made my days a few handbreaths,
> and my lifetime is as nothing in thy sight.
> Surely every man stands as a mere breath!
> (Ps 39,4–5)

When personal suffering tended to obscure the rational appreciation of existence the awareness of the temporal limits to that existence gave a much needed perspective within which the real values of life might more clearly be perceived (v. 7):

> And now, Lord, for what do I wait?
> My hope is in thee.

Man is a transient in a finite world where only God is permanent, so only in relation to him can meaning be found. True, in this psalm the poet has come to a somewhat emotional conclusion on the value of life; but Ps 49, a wisdom psalm, distils a more purely intellectual vision from the same belief. No one enjoys ultimate mastery of life or wealth; both will pass; therefore the loss of either should not inspire regrets, much less fear:

> Be not afraid when one becomes rich,
> when the glory of his house increases.
> For when he dies he will carry nothing away;
> his glory will not go down after him.
> (vv. 16–17)

The lesson is clear: concentrate on what you have — life; live that to the full while you may, for thereby one finds fulfilment.

The poet of Ps 49 shares much of his world-view with *Qoheleth (Ecclesiastes)*, but in general the more vital faith of the psalmists leads them to a different conclusion. This certainty of death can also serve to bring pressure on God — 'for in death, who will be there to praise you?' is the shrewd observation of Ps 6, and the poet thereby hopes to induce God to restore his health and prolong life.

From the point of view of religion, this appreciation of mortality had one very positive result: it placed a very high price on human life, and as a result Israel was moved to evolve a superb theology of time (see Eccles 3) and of creation (Ps 96, Ps 104). The psalmist knows that all things are in the hand of God; they exist only because he drew them out of chaos (Gen 1) and continues to hold them in being. Man, surrounded by chaotic powers that threaten the stability of his existence, will therefore praise God all the more fervently for *any* gift of life. Indeed, it becomes evident that God must have established laws for the preservation of creation (Ps 24,1–2; 93,1; 96,10). Thus 'Creation' is not just a doctrine of origins — the once upon a time formation of all that is, but an intellectual perception that what once began by decree of an eternal God now abides by virtue of his eternity:

> The earth *is* the Lord's and the fulness thereof,
> the world and those who dwell therein;
> *for he has* founded it upon the seas,
> and established it upon the rivers.

The conjunction of present continuous and past definitive here in Ps 24,1–2 is indicative. The earth that once came into being by a divine act remains in being because God continues to send the freshening rain (Ps 147,8) and the life-giving sun to make it fruitful in its seasons (Ps 74,16–17). The process of creation is continuous, because God remains always its 'maker' and his 'work' of creation is ongoing in human time.

If that is so, and it clearly is for the psalmist, then it followed as one further step in an evolving theology that man began to identify with this ongoing creativity, logically presuming that if he, man, is made 'in the image of God' then it must be his vocation to be a co-creator. The later psalms in particular, under the influence of the wisdom tradition, see man as one who, under God, continues the divine work of creation by taking responsibility for his world and its flowering. In the 'Song of the Three Young Men', a later addition to the Book of Daniel (after 3,23), man the creator becomes one who speaks the 'creative word', articulating the response of inanimate nature:

> Bless the Lord, all works of the Lord,
> sing praise to him and highly exalt him for ever.
> Bless the Lord, you heavens,
> sing praise to him and highly exalt him for ever . . .
> Bless the Lord, all waters above the heavens,
> sing praise to him and highly exalt him for ever . . .
> Bless the Lord, all things that grow on the earth,
> sing praise to him and highly exalt him for ever . . .
> Bless the Lord, you whales and all creatures . . .
> all birds of the air . . . all beasts and cattle,
> sing praise to him and highly exalt him for ever.
> (vv. 35–59)

The recurrence of a refrain ('sing praise to him . . .') after every reference to nature suggests that this was a congregational response to a leader's invitation; as if the president of the assembly named the creatures and the people 'gave voice' in their stead.

This is quite a sophisticated concept of man and his world, and one might legitimately ask, what led the Old Testament theologians to such a fresh synthesis? Simply, the power of the human mind, it would seem, and the 'divine discontent' that stirs intellectual curiosity. Man is a restless animal that is always asking 'why?' of his environment. The wisdom writers in particular reflected on the human experience of life and death; on the faith tradition of Gen 1 and man's creation in the divine image, and evolved a concept of creation and of creator that might well be called 'intellectually existential': less divine revelation than human perception and excogitation. The result is an understanding of man and his world that is both sensitive and profound.

Two psalms in particular — Ps 8 and Ps 19 — offer a logically coherent concept of human nature. Taken as complements to each other, proceeding from the same premise and according to the same logic, they offer a centre-based and cohesive portrait of man, his nature and his response to his environment.

	Ps 8	*Ps 19*
Thesis:	The glory of God experienced in creation.	The glory of God experienced in creation.
Antithesis:	The finiteness of man; a creature, limited and transient.	The sun, a glorious creature, responds to God according to its nature.
Synthesis:	Grandeur of man, and his true nature.	Man must respond according to his nature: observance of Law.

Man's Search for Self-understanding: Ps 8

Psalm 8 is technically a Hymn of Praise, yet in style as in content it is far closer to the wisdom tradition than to the liturgical. It sets out on a rational journey of investigation into the dignity of both God and man, discovering on the way the essential glory of the Creator as he is reflected in the work of his hands. Yet for all its joyful spirit of wonder and praise it is dominated from beginning to end by the firmly austere question 'what is man?' (v. 4). The structure of the psalm reflects an exercise in dialectic — an attempt at transcending the limits of the known (human experience) so as to arrive at global knowledge. This dialectic is two-sided: God's visible magnificence (v. 3) certainly implies the question 'what is man?' (v. 4) — but it might also be said to raise the question 'what is God?' and this is in fact in vv. 5–9; for if man is God's image, God's nature becomes manifest in man; if man is 'little less than God' then God is 'little more than man', and both share the same functions of 'dominion over the works of his hands' (v. 6). Heaven, moon, stars, all the glories of a perceptible creation make God visible, but man has a clear superiority over them. So what is he?

The development of biblical anthropology is very dependent on one central perception: that man is 'image and likeness of God'. This was first proposed by the priestly authors of Gen 1, and was developed along separate lines by Sirach (see chapter 17) and the author of *Wisdom* (chapter 2). So it would appear that exploration of either concept, 'God' or 'man', must result in an understanding of the other. Peeling away the layers that clothe the concept 'Creator' results in an elucidation of the divine element in 'man'. In this sense, both God and man share a common inner being. This is the starting point of Ps 8. Beginning with the known — the majesty of the Creator that may be experienced in the contemplation of his works, one confronts the unknown — man's finiteness and the limits of his glory. In this way a truly gifted poet-theologian carries his readers beyond experience to a comprehension of that great unknown.

> O Yahweh, our Lord,
> how majestic is your name in all the earth,
> you whose glory above the heavens is chanted!
> (Ps 8,1)

The psalm, a carefully structured and tightly woven unit, begins and ends with the same idea: v. 1 and v. 9 form an 'inclusion', or conceptual frame, that supplies the perspective within which the poet works and controls the development of the theme 'man and God'. This framework, in its literary setting, is the response of man to the revelation of God the Creator, here manifesting his 'name' — that is, his nature — to his subjects. The natural response — wonder and joy — serves merely to lead the reader into a more profound analysis of this 'name' as it comes to be perceived in 'all the created world' (v. 1). Verse 3 then serves as a link between the poet's first, lyrical, reaction and his subsequent theological development, marking the passage from what is perceived (vv. 1–2) to what may be apperceived (vv. 4ff).

> When I look at thy heavens, the work of thy fingers,
> the moon and the stars which thou hast established;
> What is man . . .?

The poet of Ps 8 already had the theological foundations for his elaboration ready to hand in the tradition of the Priestly Document, especially the sophisticated and highly evolved 'creation narrative' of Gen 1,26–28 — the creation of mankind according to certain categories:

> Then Elohim said, let us make man in our image, after our likeness; and let them have dominion over the fish of the sea, and over the birds of the air, and over the cattle, and over all the earth.

The later trends in Old Testament anthropology find their starting point in this theology of mankind created in God's own image and given dominion over all creation. That the author of Ps 8 evokes this tradition is evident from vv. 5–8 where man is said to have been 'made little less than Elohim . . . crowned with glory and honour . . . and given dominion' over the world. The basic ideas are clearly those of Gen 1, as is the designation of the Creator as 'Elohim' (v. 5a). In the psalm, however, human speculation takes precedence over the divine imperative. So impressed is the poet by the awesomeness of creation that he is driven to draw out the implications for man in *his* unique creaturehood. 'What is man?' is a common enough question in the psalms (see Ps 90,10 and Ps 144,3), but for Ps 8 it is no longer a pious exclamation or an acknowledgement of human finiteness; it has become a goad to intellectual curiosity. If inanimate creation so eloquently speaks the 'name' of the Creator, what must man, theologically understood, represent? Taking v. 3 as its thesis (experience of God in creation) vv. 4–6 interrogates the human dimension:

> What is man that thou art mindful of him,
> and the son of man that thou dost care for him?
> Yet thou hast made him little less than God,
> and dost crown him with glory and honour.
> Thou hast given him dominion over the works of thy hands;
> thou hast put all things under his feet.

Verse 4 offers, by implication, the necessary antithesis — man's finiteness — and both thesis and antithesis then come together in the startlingly original synthesis that is v. 5. Man is certainly a creature, but one that is separated by a mere breath from the creating godhead.

This is implicit in the language of Ps 8. The 'God' with whom man is here (v. 5a) confronted is called 'Elohim', and this is frequently thought to be ambitious, meaning perhaps 'gods' (or even 'angels'). But surely it can only mean God himself, if the poem is to maintain any inner coherence. In the first place, the term 'Elohim' is commonly used for the God of the Old Testament, and indeed Gen 1 uses it of the Creator in whose image mankind is made (Gen 1,26). In the second place, the formal inclusion of v. 1 and v. 9 refers the whole psalm to Yahweh himself, and this stylistic dominates the entire work. Moreover, Yahweh is 'our Lord' in both verses, and this title is frequently applied to God when his role of divine sovereign and master of creation is in question, as Ps 97, Ps 135 and Ps 147 attest in praising God as ruler and 'Lord' of creation.

Fearful, perhaps, that this 'new theology' might be passed over, the poet himself avoids ambiguity by using divine terminology in v. 5b. Man is 'crowned', a characteristic of God's viceroy on earth; and specifically with 'glory' and 'splendour', both attributes of the divinity — especially in self-manifestation and in his relationship to the works of his creation (Ps 19,2; 57,6.12; 72,19; 104,31). Thus Ps 8 speaks of the 'nature' of God in some way postulated of mankind; the human person making the divinity present, and representing his 'glory' as it is manifested to creation. It may be of interest to note that in varying ways both Sir 17 and Wis 2 use the same theological pattern to evolve their own particular anthropology.

This statement about man is now followed in Ps 8 by a passage that is clearly reminiscent of Gen 1 and the stewardship that the human person exercises on earth as God's 'image'. Indeed, v. 8 takes up almost verbatim the divine imperative of Gen 1,28 with which God addressed his human creatures:

> be fruitful, and multiply, and fill the earth and subdue it; and have dominion over the fish of the sea, and over the birds of the air and over every living thing that moves upon the earth.

Psalm 8,6–8 puts a slightly different emphasis on it:

> Thou hast given him dominion over the works of thy hands;
> thou hast put all things under his feet,
> all sheep and oxen,
> and also the beasts of the field,
> the birds of the air, and the fish of the sea,
> whatever passes along the paths of the sea.

Having evolved all of this, the author returns firmly in v. 9 to close the psalm with the echo of his first premise, the majesty of God:

> O Yahweh, our Lord,
> how majestic is thy name in all the earth!

It may be significant that this final verse, unlike v. 1, speaks only of the manifestation of the divine 'name' *on earth.* Heaven is not mentioned; but then, in the perspective of Ps 8 man's role as 'divine image' is restricted to the terrestrial arena where he is co-creator, and where by means of his artistic and intellectual capacity he too wrests form and meaning from the world's chaos, extending the frontiers of knowledge and of control, as Elohim himself had done (Gen 1,2) in his first creative movement.

Man's Search for a Standard of Values: Ps 19

Psalm 19 is frequently taken to be two separate psalms, and this is possible since two sections on diverse topics can be distinguished: vv. 1–6 dealing with Creation, and vv. 7–14 with the Law. Yet read as one unified psalm it presents an interesting combination of ideas that must have been significant at least for an early editor. The first half is, like Ps 8, a Hymn of Praise and it establishes the dominant motif. Since the normal function of a hymnic introduction is to initiate dialogue, one can begin to read Ps 19 with the question — what end does this 'praise' serve?

There are in fact two 'hymns of praise' — of creator and of law-giver — each having a different thrust; each complementing the other. The function of 'praise of creation' is to glorify God. Yet, being inanimate and voiceless, the heavens (vv. 1ff) cannot do this unless man is there, somehow to articulate that praise. 'Praise of the Law' serves a different end. It is clearly meant to inculcate *observance* of and respect for 'the testimony of the Lord' (vv. 7ff). The question that remains in the mind of the reader is therefore — how does Ps 19 envisage both these ends being effected?

In general, 'creation' psalms celebrate God for the creation and preservation of the world: since it has been created by God it has a splendour of its own which gives testimony. Ps 19 emphasizes this sense of witness by bringing together the two ideas of creation and law, and thus presenting, like Ps 8, a process of dialectic. But while both psalms begin with similar introductory verses the scope of Ps 19 is unique, for the introduction of 'Law' has changed the thrust. God may be experienced in two ways that determine religious response: through *nature*, which may lead to natural religion; and through *law*, which results in revealed religion. Thus while both Ps 8 and Ps 19 begin with the same *thesis*, the *antitheses* differ, and so must the syntheses. Ps 8 was concerned to establish man's *nature*, but Ps 19 complements this by using the same process of dialectic to emphasize the *ethical* response of man to the glory of God.

Already in vv. 1–2 Ps 19 casts a different light on the common thesis, which is the glory of God experienced through nature and its wonders:

The heavens are telling the glory of God;
  and the firmament proclaims his handiwork.
Day to day pours forth speech,
  and night to night declares knowledge.

What strikes one is the note of continuity, communicated by means of a series of participles: '. . . are telling', '. . . is proclaiming', '. . . is declaring'. The testimony given to God by creation is a present reality, with implications for both present and future. God has been at work (v. 4c) and still is, and his artefacts continually manifest his power. How? Through their own inherent power to communicate. Though speechless and without words (v. 3), creation still has a 'voice' that transcends the barriers of mere spoken language (v. 4), and that voice is the fact that he has placed in the heavens a sun that can be seen wherever one is on the earth. The fact that this is said, rather artificially, in v. 4c instead of where it might seem to belong (as v. 5a) is no accident, but a brilliant piece of linguistic apposition on the part of the author:

There is no speech, nor are there words;
  their voice is not heard;
Yet their voice goes out through all the earth,
  and their words to the end of the world.

  In them he has set a tent for the sun,
which comes forth like a bridegroom leaving his chamber,
  and like a strong man runs its course with joy.
Its rising is from the end of the heavens,
  and its circuit to the end of them;
  and there is nothing hid from its heat.

This is an elaboration of the introductory statement that creation speaks and imparts knowledge (v. 2). One sees the sun, under its lordly canopy of sky, and by experience comes to *know* its meaning. For there is a continuing relationship between the artefact and the craftsman: one looks at a carved image and one infers something about the carver. Neither will belong solely to the past as long as someone sees the 'work of the artist's hand' before him. A masterpiece points to a commensurate master — and see how majestic is the sun and how limitless its course (v. 6). Human language is circumscribed, and neither 'speech' nor 'words' are always capable of communicating a message. But creation's voice is not so limited — if only one has experience of it and intelligence enough to think about it. It is thus at once universally valid as a medium of communication and inarticulate without man-the-interpreter (vv. 3–4). Its 'speech' conveys meaning only where human reason makes a logical inference from the evidence it has collected and assimilated.

This hymnic first part of Ps 19 is a powerfully suggestive piece of poetry. Not only is the typical Hebrew parallelism maintained *between* the verses, but there is a subsidiary parallelism within each verse as well, and the combination is evocative. 'Day to day' parallels 'night to night', as does 'speech' and 'knowledge'; but 'day' also parallels 'day' within the same half-verse, as does 'night' and 'night'. It all adds up to a carefully written and subtly nuanced piece of poetry. The 'heavens are telling the glory of God' (v. 1a), and one is forced to ask 'how?' By the fact that 'he has set (there) a tent for the sun' (v. 4c). Once the datum of v. 4c is perceived, v. 1 has its explanation.

Verses 7–14 now add a 'praise of the Law' to that (possibly older?) creation hymn, and the strict parallelism of v. 7ab at once makes the point in the best wisdom style:

> The *law* of the Lord is perfect,
> *reviving the soul*;
> the *testimony* of the Lord is sure,
> *making wise* the simple.

Law, or as it is found in the Hebrew text *Torah*, is in fact not 'law' in the forensic sense, but rather 'instruction'; in the Old Testament it represents a set of map-readings that show the way, something that reveals the totality of God's will, not in the abstract but in concrete human situations. His 'testimony' is a clear light shed on the dark path that man must walk through life. As it occurs in the psalms (such as Pss 1, 19, and the classic 119) it frequently represents a definite moment of encounter with God in his act of self-revelation. Thus this section of Ps 19 — life according to the Law — is seen as a human response to the experience of God. In v. 7b this response is understood to be analogous to attaining wisdom, becoming a full human person in both secular and religious domains. It is characterized by 'fear of the Lord' (v. 9), which to the sages marked a stage of intimacy with Yahweh that was almost a natural and intuitive 'feeling for' his point of view. Starting from the experience of God in his creation the wise man arrives at a stage of personal intimacy:

the fear of the Lord is clean,
  enduring for ever;
the ordinances of the Lord are true,
  and righteous altogether.
More to be desired are they than gold,
  even much fine gold;
sweeter also than honey
  and drippings of the honeycomb.
(vv. 9–10)

This is seen to be the natural outcome of encounter with the God who continually communicates himself through his creation and through the revelation of his will. The more real this communication becomes, the more fully one enters into 'knowledge', and knowledge *is* experience for the psalmist, distilled and assimilated. This idea explains the sapiential tone of this second part of the psalm. For the sages 'human fulfilment' was the goal of wisdom, and in Ps 19,7–11 emphasis is placed on the fulness of human life that is the lot of those who live out the implications of God's 'Law and testimony'. This is a *process*, as it were of self-creation. If 'law' as v. 7 sees it is an expression of God's will, then the more one grows in perception the more one's sense of the divine (or 'fear' as v. 9 has it) will mature.

So Ps 19 develops its dialectic from the same starting point as Ps 8, but reaches a different conclusion. The antithesis here is the sun, a creature whose light, though majestic of itself, serves merely to indicate the greater light of its creator. Man is a less 'glorious' creature perhaps, but he has been admitted to an intimacy denied inanimate creation. If the order of the world gives witness to God how much more must man, God's intimate correspondent. Once again the emphasis comes on the implied question 'how?' The sun does so by 'running its course with joy' (v. 5) in the sight of humanity; that is, by acting according to its nature. So man must respond to God by acting according to *his* nature; and *Torah* represents the natural expression of man's created nature.

The psalm ends (v. 14) with the sort of 'ethic of interiority' that is associated with the entrance *torot* (Ps 15 and Ps 24): speech and deed that correspond; actions being truly representative of that inner dynamic that is one's vital force. Quite simply, one lives in such a way that 'the words of one's mouth' really express 'meditations of one's heart'. This is the mature religious response favoured by the wisdom writers, in which one's external behaviour flows naturally from one's quality as a human being. The psalmist has turned the *injunction* of Ps 15 and Ps 24 into a *prayer*: may I live out the implications of my created glory and a law-enlightened relationship to the Creator (v. 14):

> Let the words of my mouth and the meditations of my heart
> be acceptable in thy sight,
> O Lord, my rock and my redeemer.

The Divine 'Creative' Word

The biblical concept of God's word as 'creative' was a particular insight of Deutero-Isaiah, who may have developed it as a result of his view that God was particularly interested in the whole of his creation. It is certain that the full significance of this notion of 'creative word' is found in the later literature that deals with Yahweh as the God of heaven who maintains a relationship with the world and with man. This is a fundamental truth for the author of Ps 33, to whom God is still involved with the world he created (v. 14) and whose 'word' is still the means of communication between his dwelling place in heaven (v. 13) and the world man inhabits. Indeed, in its own way the psalm is a formal recognition of the ongoing creativity of God's 'word':

> For the word of the Lord is upright;
> and all his work is done in faithfulness.
> He loves righteousness and justice;
> the earth is full of the steadfast love of the Lord.
> By the word of the Lord the heavens were made,
> and all their host by the breath of his mouth.
> He gathered the waters of the sea as in a bottle;
> he put the deeps in storehouses.
> (vv. 4–7)

Given the hymnic form of the psalm, these verses must serve as the point of encounter that then becomes public testimony and a prolongation in time of that primal act of divine creation. The 'word' of God 'made the heavens'; by speaking it again the one who recites the psalm becomes a co-creator, once more articulating the first 'creative word' and thus speaking creation's otherwise voiceless praise. Verse 4 makes a double statement about the Creator (and thus about his work), which is then developed as God manifests, through recital, the working out of his relationship to the world.

In this way the divine attributes of 'uprightness' and 'faithfulness' that once characterized the creative act are presented again and again in time. But what is of particular importance is the fact that the hymn-form is used, for with this genre praise is never simply discursive, never sets out merely to expand a divine attribute. In fact, it is structurally austere, presenting one basic affirmation that is developed according to the personal perception of the poet. Therefore, it is to be presumed that Ps 33 presents *one* statement with *two* poles of perception. Emphasis naturally falls on v. 5b, which is the intellectual high-point of the whole psalm:

> the earth is full of the steadfast love of the Lord.

This is the starting point of the psalmist's confession of faith. But as 'faith' is an aspect of knowledge, and knowledge is based on human experience, it can only be the psalmist's experience of the created universe, and his perception that this is traceable back to the creative word (note that v. 6 is reminiscent of Gen 1 and Is 40), that stands behind the intellectual summary of vv. 8–9:

> Let all the earth fear the Lord,
> let all the inhabitants of the world stand in awe of him!
> For he spoke, and it came to be;
> he commanded and it stood forth.

Since this is so, and these verses follow on from vv. 4–7, 'fear' must be the primary human reaction to the contemplation of supreme mastery of the world, the 'wonder and joy' that Ps 8 indicated. Yet the implication of these verses is that 'fear' includes *recognition* of the unique nature of God, and a concurrent element of responsibility *to* God, and *in and to* creation itself.

There is a dimension of intellectual speculation here, a 'theology-in-the-making' element as the psalmist not only *perceives* 'nature' and postulates 'God' but connects both to 'man' and a human reaction of 'recognition'. The calm tone adopted by the psalmist suggests that one is dealing with a studied reflection on God and his handiwork . So it may be taken as 'theology-turned-prayer'; a believer quietly thinking out the implications of the traditional creation-theology. After all, the psalm is addressed to 'you righteous' (v. 1) who already stand in possession of a theological tradition; and vv. 18–19, taking up the concepts 'steadfast love' from v. 5 and 'fear' from v. 8 and then personalizing them, would seem to suggest that contemplation of God's creativity involves the faithful in the continuity of the creative event. The earth is full of the creative love of God, whose eye *is* on the one who recites the psalm. Ps 33 stands as a powerful catechesis, a witness to ongoing creation.

This idea is found in a very marked way in Ps 65, another act of 'recognition'. The structure is simple: vv. 1–4 enunciate the theological principle that God is always effective; vv. 5–10 recall his creative act of the past; and vv. 11–12 recognize how this is actualized in a feast of harvest (New Year, perhaps?). It clearly places the emphasis on vv. 5–10, the stability and continuity of creation:

> By dread deeds thou dost answer us with deliverance,
> O God of our salvation,
> who art the hope of all the ends of the earth,
> and of the farthest seas;
> who by thy strength hast established the mountains,
> being girded with might;
> who dost still the roaring of the seas,
> the roaring of their waves,
> the tumult of the peoples;
> so that those who dwell at earth's farthest bounds
> are afraid at thy signs;
> thou makest the outgoings of the morning and the evening
> to shout for joy.
>
> Thou visitest the earth and waterest it,
> thou greatly enrichest it;
> the river of God is full of water;
> thou providest their grain,
> for so thou hast prepared it.
> Thou waterest its furrows abundantly,
> settling its ridges,
> softening it with showers,
> and blessing its growth.

This blends past event and the present situation of the psalmist in one 'moment' of experience that transcends time, so that praise (v. 2) and recognition (v. 4) are now caught up in one theological statement: God *is*, and he creates. Verses 6–7 thus present creation as an ongoing experience through which man apprehends the creator, for the atemporality of the creative act reflects the timelessness of God; so the effectiveness of his 'strength', manifested once and for all, is a present reality.

Verse 5a is clearly the beginning of a theological elaboration based on experience and reason: 'by dread deeds (past creation) you answer us with (present) deliverance'. This is an intellectual tour-de-force, for it sees creation as a theophany ('dread' in v. 5a belongs to the language of divine epiphany), combining the essence of might and its manifestation, and evoking the natural human response, which in Ps 65 is 'hope' (v. 5b) and 'fear' (v. 8). This response is communicated to all the ends of the earth by the testimony of recital. God manifests his power; the psalmist, perceiving this, experiences the presence of the divinity and by his act of recognition passes this on — thus becoming himself a 'testimony', a re-sounding of the original creative word that now echoes through his world, so that the 'mountains' once established by God still stand (v. 6) for he is still moving over the 'primal waters' (Gen 1), controlling them (v. 7). Thus the psalmist's praise becomes a theophany to all the peoples who now share his experience of the creator at work as well as his reaction to that — v. 8 taking up once more the concept 'fear'.

The final verses (vv. 9–10) of this central section present the theological synthesis that derives from experience and reason. Just as he was at creation, so God still *is* with regard to the present world, and will be as long as the world subsists. It is not so much that God *created* the world as that he drew it out of chaos *and holds it in being* by means of man's repeating the 'word' by a testimony that involves others in his own experience.

The Meaning of 'Praise'

In treating these psalms in which nature is contemplated one must be careful *not* to consider them 'nature poetry' — there is no nature poetry as such in the psalter. Creation is evoked and its beauties sung only in so far as it points to its creator, and is thus part of a larger whole — the concept of divine creation itself. Latent in these hymns is a fundamental theological perspective that determines their usage. When God created the world he drew it out of chaos. That is the basic idea found in Gen 1,1–3:

> In the beginning God created the heavens and the earth.
> The earth was without form and void, and darkness was
> upon the face of the deep; and the spirit of God was
> moving over the face of the waters. And God said,
> 'Let there be light'; and there was light . . .

To the Hebrew, material creation is thenceforth held balanced over chaos by God. As long as he maintains it all is well, but should his creative 'word' ever cease to resound all would return to chaos. The recitation of the psalms that praise God for his creation become that 'spoken word', and since it is a *creative* word psalmic 'praise' both announces *and effects* creation anew. Essentially, they represent an experience of God: that of a once for all time act of creation which, by recitation, becomes an ongoing act.

In this way these psalms are a form of kerygma. When recited they both announce and effect something. Their content is thus not primarily doctrine — they do not intend as such to teach a reader *about* creation; their content is *an event or events*, so when spoken again they re-effect this event. Thus, Israel's reaction to encounter with a creator God in the psalms is a reaction to a fact, not to a doctrine. And that fact is the continuity of the creation-event. The God who is thus revealed is less a 'God who acted once' than a 'God who is', and who continues to speak a creating and revealing word.

CHAPTER 5

PSALMS OF HUMAN NEED AND DISTRESS

Human need takes many forms. It can be the savage alienation brought by physical pain or psychological stress; the loss of an intellectual basis for one's faith; the pedestrian sense of an absence of value or meaning to life. Whatever form it takes it is, for thinking man, always a catalyst. It provokes a reaction: awareness of human need is the starting point of any journey of recovery.

In the psalter this is invariably a religious perception, for God is inescapably part of any equation that can be called 'life'. Any diminution of human well-being, any loss of *shalôm*, is indicative of something gone wrong with an individual's relationship to God. The first and most immediate cure is to be found in prayer, the restoration of personal intercourse with the source of existence. Indeed, even if it must be as judge that he comes, God's presence is immeasurably better than his absence, as Ps 17,1–3 attests:

> Hear a just cause, O Lord;
> attend to my cry!
> Give ear to my prayer from lips free of deceit!
> From thee let my vindication come!
> Let thy eyes see the right!
> If thou triest my heart, if thou visitest me by night,
> if thou testest me, thou wilt find no wickedness in me;
> my mouth does not transgress.

This is formally a 'Lament', but it is also one man's studied judgement on human life and alienation, and is typical of the whole Old Testament. Pain diminishes the personality, but prayer of any sort will initiate a process of restoration. In the 'lament' type of psalm in particular it can be seen how sickness, pain or any of the burdens of mortality can in fact become an arena within which one encounters God and re-discovers *shalôm*.

Naturally, death is the great enemy of all the living, but it is particularly evident in the psalter that death is not a simple, clearly determinable moment: its domain encroaches upon life itself, casting its shadow of sickness, oppression, poverty. All of these are seen as death's outriders, manifestations of its ultimate dominion over the living. To lack anything of life's fulness was to be reduced to a state that was at best *relatively* human, and one became something of an outsider in a society that was dominated by the knowledge of life's transitoriness. This fact gives a definite emphasis to the theology of the psalms of lamentation, which serve a positive function for both individual and society. In the appeal to God, found in one way or another in all these poems, the suppliant is given a point of stability, something to hold on to; a key to meaning in what otherwise would be an alien world. He participates in a very actual way in something that never changes — the presence of an interested God. The almost invariable structure of the 'Lament' makes this obvious. There is always a clearly marked passage from 'request' to 'acknowledgement' or recognition. Sometimes the change is indicated by the use of a priestly oracle, which seems to guarantee the effectiveness of the prayer for rehabilitation, as in Ps 12,5:

> 'Because the poor are despoiled,
> because the needy groan,
> I will now arise,' says the Lord;
> 'I will place him in the safety for which he longs';

more often by a simple copulative — 'then' or 'but' — as in Ps 55, 16:

> But I call upon God;
> and the Lord will save me.

There is always a clearly defined moment of change, when an oppressive situation is reversed. The psalmist presents himself before God, opens his heart to pour out his troubles, and during the course of the prayer receives confirmation of grace; he will then end his prayer with an expression of gratitude for what is to him a *fait-accompli.*

While used in the liturgy — and many of them represent a liturgical testimony of thanksgiving — by their nature they pertain more to the realm of private life and personal difficulty, especially the kind known as 'Individual Lament'. The psychological pattern is too deeply incised to be merely ritual, and one can frequently trace a genuine personal issue behind the formal prayer. A classic example of the genre can be found outside the psalter in the two-part 'prayer of Hannah' in 1 Sam 1,9–2,10.

Technically, only the last ten verses of this story form the 'Song of Hannah', which seems to be a later addition to the story of the birth of Samuel. Yet the whole section admirably scores the dramatic movement in three acts that is found in all laments. The heroine is barren, and longs for a child. During one of her annual pilgrimages to the shrine of Shiloh she enters the 'temple of the Lord':

> After they had eaten and drunk in Shiloh, Hannah rose. Now Eli the priest was sitting on the seat beside the doorpost of the temple of the Lord. She was deeply distressed and prayed to the Lord, and wept bitterly. And she vowed a vow and said, 'O Lord of hosts, if thou wilt indeed look on the affliction of thy maidservant, and remember me, and not forget thy maidservant, but wilt give to thy maidservant a son, then I will give him to the Lord all the days of his life, and no razor shall touch his head'.
>
> (1 Sam 1,9–11)

Thus the scene is set with the first act of a typical lament, though most of those in the psalter lack any such clear description of the particular human need that calls them forth. The narrative force of 1 Sam 1–2 draws the reader into a participation with its protagonist in her 'need', and into a subsequent indentification with her in thanksgiving when, after her return home from Shiloh, 'she conceived and bore a son' (1,20). The rest of the narrative adds the second and third acts — assurance of divine intervention and act of thanksgiving (1,23b–2,5):

> So the woman remained and nursed her son, until she weaned him. And when she had weaned him, she took him up with her, along with a three-year-old bull, an ephah of flour, and a skin of wine; and she brought him to the house of the Lord at Shiloh; and the child was young. Then they slew the bull, and they brought the child to Eli. And she said, 'Oh, my lord! As you live, my lord, I am the woman who was standing here in your presence, praying to the Lord. For this child I prayed; and the Lord has granted me my petition which I made to him. Therefore I have lent him to the Lord; as long as he lives, he is lent to the Lord'.
>
> And they worshipped the Lord there.
>
> Hannah also prayed and said,
> 'My heart exults in the Lord;
> my strength is exalted in the Lord.
> My mouth derides my enemies,
> because I rejoice in thy salvation.
> There is none holy like the Lord,

there is none besides thee;
there is no rock like our God.
Talk no more so very proudly,
let not arrogance come from your mouth;
for the Lord is a God of knowledge,
and by him actions are weighed.
The bows of the mighty are broken,
but the feeble gird on strength.
Those who were full have hired themselves out for bread,
but those who were hungry have ceased to hunger.
The barren has borne seven,
but she who has many children is forlorn'.

So strong is the reader's identification with this episode that the 'Song of thanksgiving' has become a formal recital of divine intervention *on behalf of the nation*, as well as a personal prayer of gratitude. A private grief has become a communal triumph. The three constitutive elements of the lament are present, and illustrated: human need; conviction of grace received; expression of gratitude.

Lament as an Act of Confidence

In fact, the unity of salvation-history is nowhere nearer the surface of biblical prayer than in the lament: the cry of a people in travail rising up to the ear of the Lord, and the Lord 'remembering' them and answering their need. Every lament is a spiritual re-play of Ex 2,23–25:

> In the course of those many days the King of Egypt died. And the people of Israel groaned under their bondage, and cried out for help, and their cry under bondage came up to God. And God heard their groaning, and God remembered his covenant with Abraham, with Isaac, and with Jacob. And God saw the people of Israel, and God knew their condition.

In the 'Individual Lament', which is the most personalized kind, most emphasis is placed on the act of faith and confidence that is the fruit of theological speculation on that very history, and this results in a declaration of certainty that one has been heard. The grace of divine help is accepted as real, though its aspect may change from psalm to psalm.

Psalm 86 is an individual lament, the cry of one lost and alienated, and more accustomed to God's indifferent silence than his salvation — as one might guess from the repetitive style of vv. 1–6. Yet the fact is that *through the act of praying that silence* meaning has come to an absurd world:

> Thou art my God; be gracious to me, O Lord,
> for to thee do I cry all the day.
> Gladden the soul of thy servant,
> for to thee, O Lord, do I lift up my soul.
> For thou, O Lord, art good and forgiving,
> abounding in steadfast love to all who call on thee.
> Give ear, O Lord, to my prayer;
> hearken to my cry of supplication.
> In the day of my trouble I call on thee,
> for thou dost answer me.
> (vv. 2b–7)

However obscurely, God has come into that situation and no other answer is deemed necessary by the poet:

> I give thanks to thee, O Lord my God,
> with my whole heart,
> and I will glorify thy name forever.
> (v. 12)

Psalm 6 is a poem of the same type. On a first reading, what immediately comes to mind is the question, 'a lament *for what*?'; what is at stake in the mind of the psalmist? The act of special pleading in v. 5 — 'in Sheol who can give you praise?' — may perhaps be passed over as a rather pathetic human expedient at gaining God's attention, but v. 4 is important for it reflects, quite simply, the poet's need of God and his need of the institution of prayer — 'Turn, O Lord, save my life; deliver me for the sake of thy steadfast love'. The first issue therefore is clearly his relationship with God, and this throws light on the opening verses of the prayer:

> O Lord, rebuke me not in thy anger,
> nor chasten me in thy wrath.
> Be gracious to me, O Lord, for I am languishing;
> O Lord, heal me, for my bones are troubled.
> My soul also is sorely troubled.
> But thou, O Lord — how long?
> (vv. 1–3)

It is a simple cry for help. The psalmist takes refuge, not in a protest of innocence (common enough in the lament), but in the grace of God. His personal feeling of insecurity is evident: stretching out his hands to God he is none too sure how much he can expect — indeed, the broken nature of v. 3 underlines the emotional condition of the suppliant. The very fact that the immediate cause of lament is not indicated may in fact point to the inner nature of the prayer. An awareness that God seems to hold himself aloof makes it the poet's first concern not to lose this relationship, which for him represents the very essence of human existence. And, seemingly, this prayer in itself is sufficient to guarantee the restoration of intimacy, for vv. 8–10 show how the psalmist has reached an assurance that his request has been heard, and union with God restored:

> Depart from me, all you workers of evil;
> for the Lord has heard the sound of my weeping.
> The Lord has heard my supplication;
> the Lord accepts my prayer.
> All my enemies shall be ashamed and sorely troubled;
> they shall turn back, and be put to shame in a moment.

The quality of life depicted here is the reverse of what was shown in vv. 6–7, for the psalmist knows that his prayer *has already been answered.*

Psalm 13 is a more complex example of lament. It is an amalgam of the experiences of many people who have known suffering — a paradigm of human distress: a rift in the relationship with God; estrangement from the community; psychological disorder. Certainly, the emotional content of the psalm is deeper and more evident than usual — a fact that suggests the poem is a very personal expression of distress. This is immediately evident in the fourfold repetition of the cry for help that the opening verses represent:

> How long, O Lord? Wilt thou forget me forever?
> How long wilt thou hide thy face from me?
> How long must I bear pain in my soul,
> and have sorrow in my heart all the day?
> How long shall my enemy be exalted over me?
> (vv. 1–2)

This is not simply the expression of a passing sense of loss or a temporary affliction. The feeling of alienation has eaten into the very soul of the psalmist. But strangely enough, this is not the predominant mood of the psalm. The whole is dominated, structurally and theologically, by a single conjunctive particle — 'but' (v. 5a) — that links this prayer of request with an act of thanksgiving, and so marks the psalm as a theophany of grace:

But I have trusted in thy steadfast love;
my heart shall rejoice in thy salvation.

Human need and divine presence balance each other, and the polarity in fact serves to accentuate the reality of God's response to human need.

The double question that constitutes v. 1 sets the tone: the origin of the psalmist's suffering, however it be manifested, is really the absence of God. Thus *shalôm*, the fulness of human wellbeing, comes from his presence to the suppliant, and is the primary requisite — indeed often the only requisite. Certainly, the fact that the more actual human need is mentioned only in v. 2 — almost as a consequence of the situation described in v. 1 — is indicative. Though God is called on to deal with a real personal need this is not specified; the emphasis remains on the appeal for divine help. And indeed, the poem's very lack of definition on this score may point to its being a liturgical response that could be adapted to the needs of individual worshippers. What remains is the poet's need to experience God's presence. Whatever else may oppress him, the first and most urgent affliction is his alienation from God. Once God enters the arena of human suffering healing has already begun, for the divine presence is known to be the source of all human wellbeing. Verses 3–4 in fact make it clear that what is in question is man in his totality — man the spiritual-physical entity he is for the Old Testament — and thus if God considers and answers me' (v. 3) the whole person is healed.

Psalm 13 is the expression of a keen psychological insight. In the opening prayer the psalmist turned to God to articulate his need; in vv. 3–4 he prayed for divine intervention. *With this the process of healing has already begun,* for God has entered the situation. Thus 'death' in v. 3 is more than the term of human existence — it is symbolic of a life separated from God; a 'sleep', not a viable human existence. Thus in the act of lament the suppliant comes closer to God, and by the urgency of his prayer tries to importune God — for he has already become aware that if he has God he has 'life'. And so with the conjunctive 'but' of v. 5 the psalmist acknowledges the fact that his prayer has changed its thrust and is on another tack. Faith has reversed the situation and the cause of lament (vv. 1–2) has gone.

But I have trusted in thy steadfast love;
my heart shall rejoice in thy salvation.
I will sing to the Lord,
because he has dealt bountifully with me.
(vv. 5–6)

This is an extraordinarily confident statement. God is presumed to have already acted. Verse 6b uses a verbal form that implies the situation has been fully, and successfully, confronted: '. . . he has dealt bountifully with . . .' signifies the case is closed. From a request in v. 3 the psalmist has passed to a clear affirmation that divine intervention has met human need. This double-verse act of thanksgiving reflects, soberly and grammatically, a definitive gift of healing grace that the poet has personally experienced.

A Prayer of Disenchantment

The apparent silence of God, man's inability to make contact with him, and the resultant weakening of faith is a recurrent theme in biblical prayer. It is reflected in classic terms in Ps 28, which is technically a lament but might well serve as a model of prayer for vulnerable human beings. Is God interested? Will he even hear if one calls upon him? The alternative is too deadly to contemplate:

To thee, O Lord, I call;
my rock, be not deaf to me,
lest, if thou be silent to me,
I become like those who go down to the Pit.
(v. 1)

Even the subconscious fear that he *might* very well be 'deaf to me' for some reason of his own lends urgency to the psalmist's prayer as he lifts his hands in supplication:

Hear the voice of my supplication,
as I cry to thee for help,
as I lift up my hands
towards thy most holy sanctuary.
(v. 2)

These first two verses mark the psalm as a prayer addressed to God in the temple — v. 2b representing a liturgical gesture towards the Holy of Holies where God dwells among his people. Once again the reader is struck by the fact that the real concern of the psalmist is for the presence of God that is so essential to a life of faith. In fact, vv. 3–5 is a prayer for the strengthening of faith. He fears that if his mood of disillusion (caused by the seeming unwillingness of God to respond to his needs) continues he will inevitably become one of 'the wicked' (v. 3). This is a comprehensive term that has psychological rather than moral implications. They are neither atheists nor irreligious persons in the context of Ps 28. Rather, the term represents that spiritual attitude of disenchantment with religion that so easily follows on any 'dark night of the soul'. One tends to question the worth of prayer or of faith in the face of enduring silence on God's part, and thus one easily falls into an attitude of indifference.

> Take me not off with the wicked,
> with those who are workers of evil,
> who speak peace with their neighbours,
> while mischief is in their hearts.
> Requite them according to their work,
> and according to the evil of their deeds;
> requite them according to the work of their hands;
> render them their due reward.
> Because they do not regard the works of the Lord,
> or the work of his hands,
> he will break them down and build them up no more.
> (vv. 3–5)

Verse 3b shows that the 'wicked', the 'workers of evil' are simply those who, in their hearts, no longer really care about religion, but go on living behind a social façade of conformity. Thus while quite willing to accept the reality of God as an academic exercise, they refuse to allow it to have any real effect on their lives. He has become a speculative proposition rather than a person.

One certainly gets the impression that the author realized he had come close to this state of mind, and in this condition may have been capable of no more than the ritual prayer-gesture of the 'lifting of hands' mentioned in v. 2b. Yet even if he could rise no higher, the fact remains that he *has* approached God, no matter how subjectively inadequate the prayer, and this has clearly been sufficient as a first step in rehabilitation:

> The Lord is my strength and my shield;
> in him my heart trusts;
> so I am helped, and my heart exults,
> and with my song I give thanks to him.
> (v. 7)

It is possible that at some point of the liturgical act of 'prayer', perhaps after v. 5, a temple spokesman — priest or levite — delivered a ritual confirmation of grace. Whether this be so or not, vv. 6–7 quite obviously presume that the prayer, such as it was, has been heard.

> Blessed be the Lord!
> for he has heard
> the voice of my supplications.
> (v. 6)

It is like a sudden dart of sunlight, this spontaneous cry of gratitude, and it confirms the suspicion that the psalmist had not been at all sure how much he could expect from God, knowing well the state of disenchantment with religion he had reached — close as he was to joining 'those who go down to the Pit' (v. 16) as a result of God's seeming indifference to his need. What mattered, however, was less the virtue of human prayer than the divine willingness to accept will for deed and the consequent gift of encounter. On even the most fragile basis of human goodwill God can build.

The note of change in vv. 8–9, from first person to third, signals a new insight that is the result of faith recovered in adversity. The psalmist's personal experience has become a lesson for the community, to which he now can give a witness that is all the stronger for the trial through which he has passed. The introduction of the two themes 'shepherd' and 'anointed' in this last section may point to a relatively late date of composition. This would strengthen the central thrust of the psalm, since later generations in Israel, after the Exile, had singularly experienced the silence of God, and to such a community the voice of one who had come close to despair in his own life would sound with a special resonance. Whatever be the historical context, it is clear that through his meeting with God in the midst of a personal crisis of identity the poet became a sacrament of that divine 'presence-in-adversity' for the whole community.

The Abiding Nature of God's Presence

The prayer of the psalter is most clearly marked by this confidence of the divine presence in the act of supplication itself. Particularly in the formal lament this belief in the efficacy of prayer is tied, structurally and thematically, to a formal declaration of certainty of being heard by God. Assurance of his presence, and so of the efficacy of prayer, is central. For the Israelite, the prayer of human need is an arena of encounter, a quasi-infallible means of making contact with the divinity. The consciousness of human frailty, of physical or psychological isolation, is *itself* the catalyst that provokes both supplication and theophany. The actual situation of human need itself thus becomes a moment of sacramental encounter. The fact is that 'lament' is provoked by a specifically biblical concept of God: he is 'Yahweh' — the one who is present to his people at every moment of their journey through life (Ex 3, 14–15), and this is surety of both the proximity *and* the individuality of divine intervention. The psychology of the Israelite is nowhere more clearly manifested than in his attitude to personal distress, to any diminution of *shalôm* in his own life. Such deprivation drives him to pray in a very personal and emotional way, for he believes God *must* hear him. If he does not, he is being unfaithful to his own nature as God of the Covenant. Also, being the only *human* initiative possible, prayer establishes contact, and once this is effected God has entered the arena of human need. The help the suppliant requests is therefore no more than his 'right' according to the covenant promises.

In fact, Ps 14, which is a variant of a typical lament, suggests that *all* peoples of the earth are objects of God's care, and if they 'seek after him' (v. 2) may be sure of his intervention on their behalf.

> The Lord looks down from heaven *upon the children of men*,
> to see if there are any that act wisely,
> that seek after God.

The use of the universal term 'children of men' suggests a wider sphere of influence than simply Israel. In prayer, the individual inserts himself into the covenant relationship with God and thus experiences *shalôm.* The aim of the lament is thus encounter with a divinity who is known personally by his name 'Yahweh', and who is conceived of as present to the one who prays.

CHAPTER 6

THE QUEST FOR PERSONAL HOLINESS

Many of the psalms draw a clear, even at times an over-emphatic, distinction between two 'types' of people, the 'righteous' and the 'wicked', and the authors seem in no doubt as to where they themselves belong (Ps 1 and Ps 119 are examples of classification). Indeed, many of the wisdom psalms are preoccupied by this 'definition by contrast' of human goodness. But who are these people, so clearly seen by many psalmists? And far more important, what quality is it that makes them what they are? If religion is man's response to God, then what is the nature of the response required for holiness?

It is relatively easy to determine who is wicked. In Ps 10 he is the one who takes his stand on reason alone, lives by his own resources, and is as unconcerned about God as he believes God to be about him:

> Why dost thou stand afar off, O Lord?
> Why dost thou hide thyself in times of trouble?
> In arrogance the wicked hotly pursue the poor;
> let them be caught in the schemes which they have devised.
> For the wicked boasts of the desires of his heart,
> and the man greedy for gain curses and renounces the Lord.
> In the pride of his countenance the wicked does not seek him;
> all his thoughts are, 'there is no God'.
> (vv. 1–4)

This type character clearly represents the sort of person who places himself outside the sphere of God's authority, who refuses to accept his plan, and thus frustrates the divine order of things. Job is seen by Yahweh himself in somewhat the same colours, as the Creator rather astringently observes of his creature: 'Who is this that darkens counsel by words without knowledge?' (Job 38,2). But type characters are so very easy to draw, and for that reason may be accepted with some reserve. For its part, Ps 50 sees Israel as a whole in these terms, and in so doing perhaps offers a more realistic view of irreligion. The carefully structured parallel between vv. 7–11 and vv. 16–20 presents the 'wicked' as those who *practice* religion, observing all its ritual requirements, but who nonetheless tolerate, in themselves and in others, a lack of integrity, or better, of interiority:

> Hear, O my people, and I will speak,
> O Israel, I will testify against you.
> I am God your God.
> I do not reprove you for your sacrifices;
> your burnt offerings are continually before me . . .'
> But to the wicked God says:
> 'What right have you to recite my statutes,
> or take my covenant on your lips?
> For you hate discipline, and you cast my words behind you . . .'
> (vv. 7–8; 16–17)

The 'wicked' associate with those who live 'surface lives', whose observance is at best an external ritual. Such people were not exceptions to the rule in Israel, and it might well be argued by some that the Law itself supported this attitude.

Deuteronomy 23,1–6 could even be used as a defence by those whom the psalmist assails in v. 16. Here one finds a prescription of the Law of Moses that determines who shall be considered worthy to enter the presence of God:

> He whose testicles are crushed or whose male member is cut off shall not enter the assembly of the Lord.
>
> No bastard shall enter the assembly of the Lord; even to the tenth generation none of his descendants shall enter the assembly of the Lord.
>
> No Ammonite or Moabite shall enter the assembly of the Lord; even to the tenth generation none belonging to them shall enter the assembly of the Lord for ever; because thy did not meet you with bread and with water on the way, when you came forth out of Egypt, and because they hired against you Balaam the son of Beor from Pethor of Mesopotamia, to curse you. Nevertheless the Lord your God would not hearken to Balaam; but the Lord your God turned the curse into a blessing for you, because the Lord your God loved you. You shall not seek their peace or their prosperity all your days for ever.

All of the prerequisites for communion with God considered here are *ritual*: formal bodily perfection, forensic purity, a clearly discernible 'righteousness'. When one reads the story of the discovery of this 'Book of the Law' in 2 Kings 22–23 one realizes that this legal concept of holiness as 'obedience to the words of the book' (2 Kgs

22,13) reflects a particular, later, approach to *torah*. The reign of Josiah, when it all happened, was a period of reform and like many such tended to be legalistic in its definition of religion. Even some psalms share this mentality (Ps 119 for example), but many more of them have a view of sanctity that reflects a radically different, and more vital, approach to holiness.

The 'Holy Ones' in the Psalms

Once again Ps 50 can serve as an indicator — for v. 5 introduces the holy Israelite as one who is 'faithful':

> Gather to me my faithful ones,
> who made a covenant with me by sacrifice!

The term used is *hasîd*, and it occurs 21 times in the psalms. The fact that it is used in its verbal form of God himself is indicative of its quality: God 'shows faithfulness' to those who are themselves 'faithful in love' (Ps 1; Mic 6). Holiness is a matter of reciprocity, a relationship with a holy God. The last verse (23) of this psalm sums up the psalmist's view on the human quality that the term reflects:

> He who brings *thanksgiving* as his sacrifice honours me;
> to him who orders his way aright
> I will show the salvation of God!

This is clearly a way of acting that recognizes and *responds* to the divine gift of friendship.

In Psalm 30 and Ps 52 this idea is expanded. Here the godly man is one who recites psalms of thanksgiving — that is, one who has encountered divine graciousness in dialogue and response:

> Sing praises to the Lord, O you his saints,
> and give thanks to his holy name.
> For his anger is but for a moment,
> and his favour is for a lifetime.
> Weeping may tarry for the night,
> but joy comes with the morning.
>
> As for me, I said in my prosperity,
> 'I shall never be moved'.
> By thy favour, O Lord,
> thou hadst established me as a strong mountain;
> (Ps 30,4–7a)

What is in question is a way of life grounded in the consciousness of grace received, and in Ps 79, Ps 148 and Ps 149 this grace is the Covenant: the 'holy ones' are those who reflect the covenant love of God by a manner of life that demonstrates to the world *what they have become by grace.*

In classical terms, holiness is a 'way of life'. In the Old Testament this relational (and non-ritual) concept is closely linked to the idea of covenant. One free partner (Yahweh) takes the initiative and pledges himself to another. He gave himself first, and then drew the other to equally full commitment. Man responds by choosing one of the many ways he can reflect the rich variety of God's call. Observance of *torah* is a necessary element, but so is fidelity to the particular way one perceives the original grace and how it impinges upon oneself. It is a very personal affair. For only God is 'holy', and holiness in others is an assimilation of that divine quality according to each individual's perception of his being 'image of God'.

The Personal Nature of Holiness

One kind of psalm in particular demonstrates this aspect of individuality and interiority — the 'entrance liturgies', or 'entrance *torot*' of the psalter. These are liturgies that marked the Israelite's entrance into the Temple to worship, and they share a common structural pattern, being composed of three parts:

A Question: what is required of the one who seeks the presence of God?

An Answer: a listing of qualities that go to make up 'God-worthiness'.

A Blessing: pronounced by a leader as one entered into the Temple of God.

These psalms reflect a particular, religious, point of view. Law, or '*torah*', is seen in its original sense — as *instruction*: a catechesis for living that reveals the totality of God's will.

Two such psalms are 15 and 24, and the requirements for entrance to worship are here seen to be *moral*, and not ritual — as one might expect in such a liturgical context. They both inculcate a way of life, an allegiance to an ethical standard of values.

Psalm 15 is perhaps the more austerely beautiful, and its place in Judaic tradition is suggestive. In a Jewish commentary on the psalms it is said that Gamaliel wept when he contemplated the first verse alone, for ritual requirements of bodily cleanliness, and the ascetic practice of fasting and mortification, would be more easily achieved than the conditions found in the first two verses — a superb ideal, indeed, that of the holy Israelite:

> O Lord, who shall sojourn in thy tent?
> Who shall dwell on thy holy hill?
> He who walks blamelessly,
> and does what is right,
> and speaks truth from his heart.

The force of the double-phrase in the Hebrew of v. 1 is what immediately impresses a reader: 'sojourn . . . God's tent . . . dwell' evokes the nomadic lifestyle of the patriarchs, where the 'tent' was the real, family dwelling place, a place set apart where only those who were 'of the family' were to be found. Thus real co-habitation with the divine is being postulated of man. And by extension, since God is a holy God, real 'holiness' is in question. And the reader is forced to interrogate his values: what *is* goodness of life? Verse 2 begins the ritual answer in a way that leaves an indelible mark on the mind, presenting as it does a clear and comprehensive moral principle, and that principle is clearly *man's interiority as a man*, his essential nature as a human being. Thus it is immediately evident that holiness is not to be found in the observance of an ethical code imposed on the individual from without — either by man *or* God. Rather is it the natural expression of one's selfhood, the articulation of one's being 'image of God'. And so the divinely revealed ethical code that is called 'Law' is merely an expression in concrete terms of what man is by his created nature; *torah* as instruction for living. One lives out the implications of one's inner being. What v. 2 proposes is not simply an injunction to act in a given way at a given time; it is the 'colour' of one's life. 'Doing what is right' represents then more a way of being, and not just a way of acting. Once the 'heart' (v. 2b), that is, the inner personality, is whole, 'truth' will naturally result in the external forum.

The implications of this 'truth' are now spelled out in vv. 3–5b:

who does not slander with his tongue,
  and does no evil to his friend,
  nor takes up a reproach against his neighbour;
in whose eyes a reprobate is despised,
  but who honours those who fear the Lord;
  who swears to his own hurt and does not change;
who does not put out his money at interest,
  and does not take a bribe against the innocent.

This is an abridged catechism of biblical morality, and it makes more explicit the ideal contained in v. 2. It is dominated by one's attitude to one's fellow creature, that is, by life in society. Again, the basic principle applies: one's attitude to others is simply the expression of one's own inner integrity. Here 'truth' is the first requisite, as indeed it must also be in one's relationship with Yahweh. 'Friend' and 'neighbour' are parallel terms here in v. 3, and are not meant to be exclusive; the whole indicates a particular attitude towards the larger community. 'Neighbour' in the older psalmic texts has not got the limited significance it tended to assume in later Judaism. Rather, it embraces all those who share a common human nature, as Ex 23,4–5 makes clear:

> If you meet your enemy's ox or his ass going astray, you shall bring it back to him. If you see the ass of one who hates you lying under its burden, you shall refrain from leaving him with it, you shall help him to lift it up;

for such an 'enemy' is in a very real sense a 'fellow human being'. Here it is evident how the psalm tries to 'interiorize' the prescriptions of the Law, emphasizing the inner nature of the human response to God. It does so again in v. 5:

> who does not put out his money at interest.

What seems to contemporary eyes a rather irrelevant precept is, in the context of Ps 15, a highly humane insight into life. In the psalmist's own society one borrowed, quite simply, because one was in need. To exploit such a situation for gain was tantamount to 'using' a fellow human being as an 'object' of one's own self-interest. This also is an emphasis on the interior dynamic of *torah*, as evidenced by Ex 22,25–27 which inculcates just such an attitude of concern for human need.

> If you lend money to any of my people with you who is poor, you shall not be to him as a creditor, and you shall not exact interest from him. If ever you take your neighbour's garment in pledge, you shall restore it to him before the sun goes down; for that is his only covering, it is his mantle for his body; in what else shall he sleep? And if he cries to me, I will hear, for I am compassionate.

The same spirit of 'common decency' is found also in Deut 24,10–15. Once again the psalmist has focused attention on the inner virtue of humanity that warms the particular external action, rather than on the forensic aspect of *torah* as 'law'.

The psalm ends with what may be an inclusion with v. 1:

> He who does these things shall never be moved.
> (v. 5c)

Thus the movement in question may be with regard to communion with God: moral goodness will ensure the continuity of one's intimacy with Yahweh, and this in itself is the only recompense to be desired.

Psalm 24, also an 'entrance *torah*', presents all the elements of a liturgical dialectic of knowledge and ignorance. Structurally, it is more complex than Ps 15, yet in essence it presents the same dialogue-structure of question and answer. Here, however, they are placed in a wider setting, and thus 'holiness of life' is given a more determined context: the created universe and the epiphany of divine holiness it represents (vv. 1–2 and 7–10).

> The earth is the Lord's and the fulness thereof,
> the world and those who dwell therein;
> For he has founded it upon the seas,
> and established it upon the rivers.
> (vv. 1–2)

This processional hymn to God the Creator establishes the parameters of the ethical requirements that follow. Creator and created are set opposite each other, and the relational aspect of created 'wholeness': it is a matter of contrast — God's holiness and man's; a concern to see oneself always in the context of Yahweh's majesty and holiness. Sharing in this is what, alone, constitutes sanctity. A sense of awe at the possibility of there being such a relationship pervades the poem, as well as a shrewd awareness of the element of 'grace' and obligation — man's goodness is an appreciation of God's gift; a response to awareness of his own created nature; a moral obligation to 'live up to' the Creator.

The nature of this holiness becomes explicit in vv. 3–6, which forms an 'entrance *torah*' similar to Ps 15:

> Who shall ascend the hill of the Lord?
> And who shall stand in his holy place?
> He who has clean hands and pure heart, –
> who does not lift up his soul to what is false,
> and does not swear deceitfully.
> He will receive blessing from the Lord,
> and vindication from the God of his salvation.
> Such is the generation of those who seek him,
> who seek the face of the God of Jacob.

Verse 4 begins the poet's analysis of the sanctity of the creature, and is effectively a re-interpretation of the *torah* of Lev 19,2: 'you must be holy, for I, your God, am holy'. This is the most fundamental demand — personal holiness. And this is quite simply a matter of 'clean hands and a pure heart' — moral actions resulting from an inner quality of goodness; human performance that is the expression of inner wholeness. The practical aids to this end are once again truth and fair dealing with others. The two 'negative precepts' of v. 4b simply exclude *all* forms of doubtful practice regarding oneself, one's neighbour or God. This much said, man is for the rest perfectly free to live out his created state in utter liberty: relate to God, and thereafter 'do what you will'.

What is evidently in question in this central section of Ps 24 is a *personal* ethic that imposes nothing extraneous to one's creatureliness: no positively stated rules of thumb, no apodictic directives. Quite simply, it envisages an integrity of conscience that naturally results in an outward integrity of act; a psychological awareness of how it is one's inner attitude that really determines what one does. This, however, is no simplistic 'liberal ethic'. It clearly presumes responsibility to a known God (vv. 1–2), and thus a personal responsibility to *know* the implications of religion and to implement them. This remains in the background, however — presumed though not stressed. What is evident is the fact that to a great degree this psalm, like Ps 15, leaves the decision to the reader. What are *your* dispositions? It is, after all, *your* life with God. One is not asked to conform to any particular type of holiness; simply, can one genuinely approach, and live with, the God of vv. 1–2? Man's way of life is dependent on his union with this God, and it is not a communal responsibility, but a personal one.

Psalm 26 adds a further dimension to the quest for personal holiness. Technically, a 'Lament of an Innocent Sufferer', the *apologia* it presents is based on a presumption of innocence — therefore it stands as a definition of purity, a fitness to stand before God. The psalmist sees himself as one who is 'set apart' from the wicked, holding himself aloof from their ways (an idea already raised in Ps 50). The setting is, again, liturgical — a gesture of holiness in which the suppliant's only claim is that he has preserved his personal integrity intact:

> Vindicate me, O Lord, for I have walked in my integrity,
> and I have trusted in the Lord without wavering.
>
> (v. 1)

It is this that constitutes holiness, allied as it is to 'trust in the Lord'. But this last idea of v. 1b alerts the reader to a new perception. Here in Ps 26, to a degree not found in Ps 15 or Ps 24, one sees the *person* behind the quest, and shares the psychological tensions and moods that mark man's path to God:

> O Lord, I love the habitation of thy house,
> and the place where thy glory dwells.
> Sweep me not away with sinners,
> nor my life with bloodthirsty men,
> men in whose hands are evil devices,
> and whose right hands are full of bribes.
>
> (vv. 8–10)

This makes one thing clear: the search for God, and intimacy with him when it is achieved, is no more plain sailing than any other human relationship. Even when one has gained the desire of the heart, one can be very unsure of holding it.

The Reality of God

All of these psalms that deal with holiness share one common feature: in them the individual is forced to accept the *fact* of God, and thus to make a personal decision knowing this will inevitably affect the way he lives. He will find his place in the ranks of the 'wicked' (Ps 50,16), the self-sufficient to whom God is unreal; or he will become *hasîd*, a holy person, in his inner being.

In what, then, does 'holiness' consist for the psalmist? Given the fact that the legalistic tendency in Judaism came late on the Hebrew scene — the emphasis on 'law' being post-exilic — it is clear that the dominant religion of the psalms is much less a matter of legal observance than an individual attitude to life. Here 'law' remains *torah*, a gracious illumination given by God for man's welfare; and thus morality is a response to God's 'faithful love' (*hesed*) rather than to a set of rules. Particularly in such psalms as 111 and 73 religious observance is a joyous response to a divine gift of self:

> Praise the Lord!
> I will give thanks to the Lord with my whole heart,
> in the company of the upright.
> (Ps 111,1)

Thus, when the psalms speak of someone being 'holy', what is envisaged is less the observance of a clearly defined code than some *quality* these people possess, some inner dynamic that determines their response to God and that colours their lives. Thus it is understood as a personal relationship that can be assessed only as between two people — the individual and his God — and is therefore not subject to any external 'measuring-rod' of observance. What is more important is the fact that holiness is a matter where *being* has primacy over *doing*, interiority over conforminty. It is simply the expression of the person, and thus involves the whole man. One responds to God as oneself, with the gift of oneself. Holiness is as natural as breathing.

CHAPTER 7

THE INNER NATURE OF PRAYER

In the biblical tradition God is a personal God. This determines not only the language of prayer but its inner meaning. It becomes a relationship with another being who may be addressed, in human language, as someone who shares to some extent the human attributes of perception and passion. It also makes its own demands, for every human relationship implies some concession to 'the other', and is circumscribed by one's inability totally to understand that 'other'.

Several factors play an important role in biblical prayer. The dialogue relationship that nourishes its roots was established by God at Sinai, where he made a covenant with *some* people. Thus the grounds for dialogue are found in the divine purpose behind this act, and this inevitably leads to an element of élitism: for Israel, though not for others, prayer is primarily oriented towards God and *his* will. Its dynamic is always Yahweh's lordship over the individual. Covenant fixes the terms of mutual responsibility and so determines the parameters of dialogue. It is on the basis of special vocation that the Israelite addressed himself to God. Thus, for one elected in covenant prayer is frequently a search for the God of Exodus; its primary axis that experience that established the relationship, and its primary function the working out of the divine purpose. Like the covenant from which it springs, prayer is essentially a service, and it makes demands on *both* partners.

It is with a clear perception of origins, then, that the psalter centres the prayer-life of Israel on the Exodus experience — for the growth of all religious life is theologically an encounter with that act of divine self-revelation, and a consequent journey through the wilderness towards a goal at best obscure. It is due to this element of the unseen, this need to 'learn about' the God-man relationship, that the psalmists' prayer reflects an inner tension, a polarity of confidence of God's presence and fear that he may remain deaf to one's needs. This is particularly evident in the fact that while God is praised for his loving kindness and mercy, these are not experienced as divine 'attributes' but as elements of tension: he 'turns to man', but this may be perceived as an invasion of man's autonomy and a demand made on his service.

The Search for God and His Ways

Frequently, then, prayer (even the 'Hymn of Praise') is seen as a search for God's will and for the strength to accept it. Such is Ps 25 which, though technically a Lament, is concerned with the author's *need to know* — both Yahweh's own 'truth' and the way this particular individual should search for it. The central section from v. 10 to v. 14 suggests that it was recited in the context of a covenant festival of 'Weeks' and this serves as the author's articulation of *his* search for the meaning the covenant relationship has for him. In effect, it is a search for the meaning of vocation, one that has been brought into question by life's humiliations (v. 3). Three main ideas, and their sequence, establish the psalm as a prayer that is primarily a quest for God's way and for the strength to walk it:

vv. 4–5: 'make me *know* your ways'. In the light of vv. 1–3 it seems that these have been obscured.

vv. 8–9: though sometimes I lose sight of journey's end;

vv. 12–14: yet I can rely on the covenant relationship to keep me to your paths.

The three opening verses of the psalm establish the fact that the author both knows God and is close to him. Nonetheless, experience of his own darkened understanding makes him realize that he cannot preserve this relationship unaided — he needs Yahweh's guidance if he is to maintain his progress along life's often perplexing 'paths', as seen in vv. 4–5:

> Make me to know thy ways, O Lord; teach me thy paths.
> Lead me in thy truth, and teach me,
> for thou art the God of my salvation;
> for thee I wait all the day long.

Even to the just man the ways of holiness are not always clear, for faith — that is, 'waiting loyally on God' (v. 3) — is neither easily established nor, once established, readily maintained. The ebb and flow of this relationship, and the need of God's continued grace, is reflected in the body of the psalm where the poet finds, loses and finds again the thread of the relationship. Three times this 'righteous man' (v. 21) feels it necessary to ask for forgiveness (vv. 7, 11 and 18) and for light. The end of the journey of faith is not reached without effort, for the 'way' is often obscured by human incomprehension. If it is achieved at all it is only because God seeks it all the while the psalmist is searching for it.

> Good and upright is the Lord;
> therefore he instructs sinners in the way.
> He leads the humble in what is right,
> and teaches the humble his way.
> All the paths of the Lord are steadfast love and faithfulness,
> for those who keep his covenant and his testimonies.
> (vv. 8–10)

The poet may not always be able to *perceive* the action of God in his life, as witness vv. 2–3, 16–18 and 19–20; at best he may be granted no more than a fleeting sight of it, vv. 6, 8 and 14; yet he is capable of making a formal 'act of faith' in v. 10. This is a confessional statement, and not simply an expression of hope. It reflects a knowledge based on tthe historical experience of the covenant community (note how it occurs in oracular form in Ps 85,9–10).

What quite clearly marks Ps 25 is the fact that his moods alternate between acknowledgement of inadequacy and confession of faith. Time and again a prayer of anxiety is followed by an act of confidence in the perennial value of the covenant relationship. And it seems as if with each consecutive 'credo' he finds his feet more firmly, as for example when the simple hope of v. 5b becomes the formal invocation of the covenant in vv. 14–15:

> Thou art the God of my salvation
> and for thee I wait all the day long . . . (v. 5b)

> The friendship of the Lord is for those who fear him,
> and he makes known to them his covenant.
> My eyes are ever toward the Lord,
> for he will pluck my feet out of the net (vv. 14–15).

This marks a progress from 'prayer' to theological affirmation. To express the attitude of the psalms in general two words are used: to 'wait for' God and to 'trust in' him. Both are used in Ps 25, and together they present a picture of the soul reaching out to a God who himself has already begun the process of leading that soul (see Ps 37,7; 39,7; 42,1; 62,1–6 and 63,1).

At the other end of the spectrum of human emotion is Ps 16, a more tranquil, almost formal, recognition of God's primacy in an individual's life. Though it is not meant to be one, v. 3 is in fact a self-portrait:

> As for the saints in the land, they are the noble,
> in whom is all my delight.

Unquestionably, the author is one of 'the saints' and is consequently quite relaxed in his relationship with God — to the extent that he can say with simple confidence that 'the lines have fallen for me in pleasant places' (v. 6a): a scholar, one feels, a gentleman and a man of genuine holiness. And all of this is reflected in his prayer, which seems to be a way of life rather than a pious exercise, and is clearly founded on personal experience of the divine presence:

> Preserve me, O God, for in thee I take refuge.
> I say to the Lord, 'thou art my Lord;
> I have no good apart from thee'.

This breathes the same atmosphere as the 'entrance *torot*', and bespeaks an attitude of almost total interiority (cf. Ps 24). Even the restrained ritual 'cursing' element of v. 4 fails to break the mood. It also suggests a very civilized man behind the poem. For such a one, prayer is the natural expression of the person: an unbroken, calm contemplation of the God whose presence breaks naturally into his thoughts at all times and in every situation:

> I bless the Lord who gives me counsel;
> in the night also my heart instructs me.
> I keep the Lord always before me;
> because he is at my right hand, I shall not be moved.
> (vv. 7–8)

Life is lived, quite without fuss or strain, in the sight of God, and is the natural expression of the intimacy and interiority that is born of such communion. Thus once the 'atmosphere' of prayer is established even death — that great disrupter — cannot destroy human fulfilment:

> Therefore my heart is glad, and my soul rejoices;
> my body also dwells secure.
> For thou dost not give me up to Sheol,
> or let thy godly one see the Pit.
> (vv. 9–10)

This is a factor that plays an important role in Israel's prayer:

since God is 'God of the living' prayer must find its resonance here in this world and in human terms. Its object must to some extent be *human* well-being, and ideally should result in the perfect realization of the natural life. Thus material goods are not of indifferent value: as gifts of God they have a religious worth. Prayer, then, may be expected to lead to a fully integrated humanity.

For the poet who wrote Ps 16 it clearly did so. But, like any relationship, prayer knows its particular tensions, and many psalms speak of this. Ps 62 is one, for it represents a God who keeps pushing, who seems to be insatiable in his demands, and who never allows one rest for very long at whatever level of 'righteousness' one has attained. Whatever man had expected to achieve in terms of relationship, God seems to have other ideas.

A Prayer of 'Tranquillity': Ps 62

A preliminary reading of the psalm will make two factors emerge: one notes the obvious 'refrain' (vv. 1–2 and 5–6) that stamps this as a 'prayer of quiet'; yet the marked change of atmosphere found in vv. 9–12 calls for a re-assessment of the word 'quiet'. These two tonalities make it feasible to divide the psalm into two sections — a diptych hinged on v. 8.

vv. 1–7: peace and turmoil alternate in the poet's heart (1–4) until a level of serenity is attained (5–7);

v. 8: presents what may be called the 'vocational value' of an experience of alienation;

vv. 9–12: is a sapiential reflection on 'confidence' in prayer.

Verses 3–4 stand out as the only discordant note, the only description of adversity, and so mark the whole poem as a 'Lament' on the perfidy of 'false friends'.

The first two verses are evidently confessional — a formula that determines the development of the psalm:

For God alone my soul waits in silence;
from him comes my salvation.
He only is my rock and my salvation,
my fortress; I shall not be greatly moved.

The word used for 'silence' in the original really means 'tranquillity', 'peace of mind' and not the more common *shalôm* of personal fulfilment. It is the serenity that only God can give — a gift, and not something to be achieved by human effort. The indicative form of the first verse shows that what is in question is not a hope, nor a wish, but an actual state: 'yes, my soul is *now* at peace, but only because it is finally focussed on God alone' (v. 1a). One senses the inner strength that enabled the poet overcome some painful experience. One word in v. 1a — here translated 'for', but more correctly from the Hebrew 'truly' or 'indeed' — manifests the inner peace that comes, not *after* trial, but *in* trial; a sigh of relief no less grateful for being transitory. The poet has reached an emotional plateau in his relationship and realizes it is only a plateau. There is a long way to climb yet. Being grounded on the human struggle that is discussed in the following verses it asserts, with convincing force, the belief that tranquillity can be found in one's relationship to God, but only if God as well as man is seeking it. In a way, these verses underline the subjective dimension of faith—abandoning other expedients the author has concentrated his faculties on God in prayer, and has found peace. But what kind of peace? Certainly not affective serenity, for there follows vv. 3–4. Rather, he has acquired the *theological apparatus* needed to sustain peace on a *real*, two-person level. He has not only discovered God but has come to realize, empirically, *what God is in himself* — rock, salvation and fortress (v. 2). Thus while faith is still *essentially* subjective, the *objective* grounds for its development are already perceived.

It is here that the discordant two-verse section fulfills its structural role:

> How long will you set upon a man
> to shatter him, all of you,
> like a leaning wall, a tottering fence?
> They only plan to thrust him down from his eminence.
> They take pleasure in falsehood.
> They bless with their mouths, but inwardly they curse.
> (vv. 3–4)

This may be seen in terms of a personal interlude as the poet dramatically recalls his frustration, still very real to him and still part of his situation. The tone of grievance in v. 4b makes it clear that this was caused by something very close to the bone — the conduct of those who claimed friendship but offered enmity. And it is evidently not something he expects will pass — v. 3b sounds very like a moment of *awareness of self*; a self-assessment, a dramatization of his own sense of failure when his aberrant personality played enemy to his spiritual progress.

However, v. 4 does show a growing detachment, marked by a grammatical change to third person, from the self-focused attitude of v. 3.

Verses 5–6 now introduce a new idea, the change marked by the refrain — a modification of vv. 1–2. The use of 'hope' in v. 5b in place of 'salvation' in v. 1b shows a growth in theological awareness.

> For God alone my soul waits in silence,
> for my hope is from him.
> He only is my rock and my salvation,
> my fortress; I shall not be shaken.

From Exodus as a past, historical event of salvation the poet passes to 'exodus' as a basis for present faith; and though the external circumstances of life may remain unimproved (v. 3b) some new, inner dimension has been added. 'Hope' is what now dominates his existence. It is in the ascendant, rising like a small star into a dark sky; the darkness now suffused — even if dimly — by a 'light' that affords him a clarity of vision and so a certain stability. It is noticeable that he does not speak of his personal problems being resolved — they are still there (v. 9) for that is part of living; but they no longer determine his attitude. What does? The structural tension of the psalm leads the reader to v. 7 — God.

> On God rests my deliverance and my honour;
> my mighty rock, my refuge is God.

He has passed from a preoccupation with personal trials to a preoccupation with God.

It is at this point that the focus shifts, with v. 8 standing both as a term (to vv. 1–7) and as a new beginning (to vv. 9–12).

> Trust in him at all times, O people;
> pour out your heart before him;
> God is a refuge for us.

Theologically, this marks the passage from *poet as individual* to *poet as sacrament*. He is now a sign to 'the congregation': God *my* refuge (vv. 1–7) is now, through the poet's recitation, God *your* refuge.

As far as Ps 62 is concerned this is the 'serenity' to be expected from prayer: acceptance of the dimension of service that the covenant relationship implies. The psalmist has come to realize that communion with God is not a refuge to which one can fly for consolation in time of trial — although it seems probable that he has found some such relief. Rather, it results in a theological awareness that prayer is a single dynamic that transforms the situation *for others.* It can bring meaning to an experience of pain; it does not necessarily relieve it.

It is natural that, in this light, the rest of the psalm becomes almost exclusively didactic — the sufferer become teacher. So in vv. 9–12 the hard edge of personalism is modified and the author embarks on a more objective meditation on the effects of prayer as it influences human life. In the presence of God one adopts a standard of values different to that which normally applies in secular life. One's self-interest shrinks into relative unimportance, becoming a 'breath' that is scarcely worth bothering about (v. 9a). As a consequence a new truth emerges — one cannot rely on self, for the self cannot be the object of faith. In the last resort, it is the divine perspective on life that must serve as a scale of values.

The last two verses re-assert a principle that is now all the more academically valid because it is the fruit of personal experience: a revelation of the nature of God. This the psalmist can present to the community with all the force of a divine oracle, and it leads the reader into a series of personal conclusions on the nature of religion, ranging from simple trust to articulate, lived faith.

> Once God has spoken;
>   twice have I heard this:
> that power belongs to God;
>   and that to thee, O Lord, belongs steadfast love.
> For thou dost requite a man according to his works.
>
> (vv. 11–12)

At this particular stage of self-awareness to which prayer has led, at which only one reaction of faith is in any real way useful, it may be of value to take another look at the psalm and make a more cerebral evaluation of its meaning as a poetic unit. Two things stand out: the spontaneous personal reaction that is represented by v. 1; and the theological scaffolding then erected around this by vv. 2, 6 and 7. When viewed from this vantage point the overall picture emerges with greater clarity.

He only is my rock and my salvation,
my fortress; I shall not be greatly moved.
(v. 2)

The psalmist has begun his perception of God as 'rock' at its most immediate level of significance: God as a warrant of security. This supplies a speculative buttress to his visceral faith (v. 1). Theology, here, is rising from the human situation of spiritual frustration in an effort at clarification, and this sends the reader back to v. 1, to look at it with new eyes:

my personality is at peace
only if I (set out to) wait on God.

Then the second step in the articulation of faith — its expression in lived words — arises from the existential situation and becomes the *fruit* of prayer rather than prayer itself. On its own terms the text reflects this, showing how the 'change of tack' effects something for the psalmist: he is still 'oppressed by his enemies' of doubt (one notes how this runs, a living thread, through the psalm: vv. 3, 4, 9,10), but he has (seemingly) been lifted out of this mood *to the extent* that he can see and appreciate the other face of prayer — the reality of God — which now becomes the one reality (v. 8c).

One can easily see beyond the words of the psalm to the situation of the psalmist. From a human mood of frustration he has been raised, one suspects by a combination of grace and native wit, to a new 'faith' that is all the more solid for being realistic.

As is frequently the case with the psalms, what one finds is a faith based on a personal, and therefore unique, experience. But given the logic of language, one can often infer the process of discovery. Certainly here in Ps 62 trust in God and peace with him (vv. 1, 2, 5, 6, 7, 8 and 12) sounds the dominant note, and is probably the device by which the poet mastered his sense of sterility and, more, gained a clearer perspective on life and an unshifting foothold that not only brought him a measure of personal tranquillity but made him, by reason of his experience, a sacrament of God's presence for others (vv. 9–10). This is evident in the text itself, for vv. 1–8 demonstrate a trust and confidence hard-won in adversity, whereas vv. 9–12 echo the classic tone — calm and intellectually assured — of wisdom. Emotion and experience have given way to a 'serenity' that is realistic.

Psalm 17 shares something of the same outlook on prayer. The act of conversing with God is seen as the articulation of an interior goodness, as v. 1b attests:

> Give ear to my prayer,
> which comes from lips free from deceit;

yet this consciousness of integrity does not always result in a perceptible calm, as vv. 8–12 acknowledge:

> Keep me as the apple of the eye;
> hide me in the shadow of thy wings,
> from the wicked who despoil me,
> my deadly enemies who surround me.
> They close their hearts to pity;
> with their mouths they speak arrogantly.
> They track me down; now they surround me;
> they set their eyes to cast me to the ground.
> They are like a lion eager to tear,
> as a young lion lurking in ambush.

Given the kind of psalm that it is, the 'Lament of an Innocent Accused', these verses are most likely a form of dramatization that presents the inner tension experienced by a 'righteous man' in the face of personal affliction. The stock figure of 'the enemies', represented here by the 'wicked who despoil me' — repeated as the theme is in vv. 4b, 7, 9–12 and 13 — stands for the personal disorientation experienced by one whose prayer seems not to have any perceptible effect on his situation, yet who 'knows' as a matter of faith that God is nonetheless close to him.

As a final word on the inner nature of Old Testament prayer perhaps Ps 130,5–6 says all that needs to be said:

> I wait for the Lord, my soul waits,
> and in his word I hope.
> My soul waits for the Lord,
> more than watchmen for the morning,
> more than watchmen for the morning.

No more poignant reminder is needed that biblical prayer is at its very centre a *response* to a past divine act of self-revelation and a 'waiting on' a future revelation of divine will. It is always this divine will for the suppliant that dominates, and indeed the *Shema* of Israel — her most representative invocation — is itself an act of recognition that finds its expression in prayer. Prayer is a 'waiting on God', but how he is going to reveal himself, and what he proposes for the suppliant, remains his initiative.

CHAPTER 8

INTIMACY WITH GOD

One thing at least the psalmist knew: God could be discovered in prayer. This faith was based not on sentiment but on a theological tradition of long standing. Yahweh's 'nearness' to his people had been guaranteed in Ex 3 and in Deut 4,7:

> For what great nation is there that has a god so near to it as the Lord our God is to us, whenever we call upon him?

He is always among his own, and he wishes to communicate. For Israel, this was objective truth, and they could point to their own historical experience to substantiate it. The psalmists, for their part, take up this theology of God and by deepening a sense of nearness to him to the point where he is 'possessed' in a strikingly human way. Being essentially revelation in prayer-form the psalms arrive at a knowledge of God by responding to his initiative of self-communication. This is dialogue, and in the movement of prayer one comes to know God as one's companion in covenant and in life — and this to the degree that 'prayer' becomes the most integrated form of 'communion', where the whole person — mind, heart and body — engages in an intimate union of being.

God's 'Goodness' to the Righteous

Psalm 73 is a wisdom psalm, but it sounds a note of urgency that is unusual to the genre. The reason is that the intellectual problem of traditional theology is compounded by a personal crisis of faith. Conventional belief in a 'just' God and a world well-governed comes into conflict with the obvious fact that life, as experienced, too often seems mad and dislocated: the just suffer, and the wicked prosper in the sight of the community. This is a common enough problem in the psalter, and can be found in Ps 37, Ps 49 and elsewhere in the Old Testament, but what gives it a particular edge in Ps 73 is the fact that it is precisely in the psalmist's *own* life that faith and reason collide. How can it be possible to maintain one's confidence in, let alone one's intimacy with, such an abitrary and irresponsible deity?

Truly God is good to the upright,
to those who are pure in heart.
But as for me, my feet had almost stumbled,
my steps had well nigh slipped.
For I was envious of the arrogant,
when I saw the prosperity of the wicked.
(vv. 1–3)

The opening verse is a declaration of traditional faith, and thus of the psalmist's religious heritage: 'Indeed, God *is* good to the upright' — the Hebrew text allows no shading. This is *the* faith — the only one he knows. And this fact, so clearly stated, forces a particular logic upon the reader, expressed almost syllogistically in the first person:

God *is* good to the upright;
I know myself to *be* upright;
therefore God is good to me.

But the problem is, that while the psalmist is existentially upright, he clearly does not prosper either materially or psychologically:

All in vain have I kept my heart clean
and washed my hands in innocence.
For all the day long I have been stricken,
and chastened every morning.
(vv. 13–14)

Therefore the premise 'God is good' must have a meaning that is not immediately evident, and this meaning must be found somewhere in the psalm, unless the author is playing with his readers. The only answer given, if answer it be, is found in vv. 17–28.

Verse 17 is the turning point on the psalmist's journey of faith:

until I went into the sanctuary of God;
then I perceived their end.

But what is the meaning of the phrase in 17a — 'until I went into the sanctuary of God'? This is clearly the source of his wisdom, the point where once more reason prevails and he begins to live again and recover his lost relationship with the faith of his forebears. Unfortunately for the reader the meaning remains obscure, and all one can do is guess: a liturgical experience of God in the temple, perhaps?; a private relevation in prayer?; encounter through the word of scripture? Any one is possible, but the text allows no certainty. However, given the fact that the text is a carefully framed poetic unit *some* meaning must come across to the reader for whom it is intended. It clearly suggests some personal experience of God that makes the poet change his understanding of the concept 'prosperity' and thus re-think the 'end' of both wicked and just (v. 17b), the goal of human life. In some personal way it must demonstrate how man's 'end' has an inner meaning that goes beyond the terminology of piety. But how and where is this seen in Ps 73?

The next strophe that takes up this positive element of divine experience is vv. 21–26:

> When my soul was embittered,
> when I was pricked in heart,
> I was stupid and ignorant,
> I was like a beast toward thee.
> Nevertheless I am continually with thee;
> thou dost hold my right hand.
> Thou dost guide me with thy counsel,
> and afterward thou wilt receive me to glory.
> Whom have I in heaven but thee?
> And there is nothing upon earth that I desire besides thee.
> My flesh and my heart may fail,
> but God is the strength of my heart and my portion for ever.

The first two verses prepare the reader for a new idea, with v. 22b establishing the perspective — 'I was like *a beast* toward thee' is a very sapiential insight. Bitterness of soul (v. 21) and alienation from faith had reduced the psalmist to the level of 'animal' because it had deprived him of his proper relationship to God. Clearly, then, possession of God is seen to be the only quality that can truly be thought of as 'human', that constitutes humanity. This recalls the theology of Gen 2,7, where the 'breath of the divinity' differentiates man from the rest of the animal creation, effectively constituting him a 'human' being. What is in question, then, in Ps 73 is a theological point of view that recognizes the deprived or 'unfinished' nature of life without God, and so sees Yahweh as that which gives a 'fourth dimension' (of human-ness) to life. This perspective dominates vv. 23–26. Real 'prosperity' is found in union with God, and not in merely material riches. It is thus a question of *faith as experience* and *faith as appearance*: God, reality experienced, is *known* to be the true reality, and the rest is mere appearance — peripheral to human living.

Essentially, these verses would seem to be a record of a personal and even mystical experience, and must be grasped as such. This, then, is the way vv. 23–26 interpret v. 17. Given the Hebrew text, perhaps the best translation might be the following:

> Nevertheless, I am continually *with you*;
>   you hold me by the hand.
> You guide me with your *counsel*,
>   and will clothe me with *your own glory*.
> For me, what is there of value in heaven except you?
>   or even on earth, *except your being with me*?
> My flesh and my heart may fail,
>   but God is the strength of my heart
>   and my portion for ever.

The opening of v. 23 indicates the author's particular intention and determines the sense of the whole section — 'nevertheless'. Almost a classic description of 'religious faith' — a holding on, however grimly, to a positive relationship when reason is no longer a support. In a waterless desert one 'nevertheless' lives on, tenaciously; for there is *nothing* left if life is surrendered. What results from this attitude in Ps 73 is a faith that no longer *needs* law or liturgy; it has become a personal conviction based on an experience of God gained by the 'prayer of human need'. In fact, vv. 2–16 are almost classically 'lament-type' psalmody.

Whatever the experience was — and the inadequacy of the text allows no apodictic declaration — it was certainly more than the simple presence of God such as one would find in the liturgy. The language, with its double particle in Hebrew, 'with you/with me' (v. 23 and v. 25), is far too intense for that. It suggests a truly intimate experience, in which one possesses God and is possessed by him: 'I am continually *with you* (v. 23a), and *being with you* I am left with no desire for anything else' (v. 25b). Some authors hold that v. 24b suggests that this union is to take place after death, when the psalmist is 'received to glory'. But the word 'glory' in the Hebrew of the Old Testament (*kabôd*) does not have that sort of *local* significance, and this is especially true of the construction of v. 24b. In the psalms (as for example Ps 8) it represents rather the manifestation of Yahweh, his *kabôd*, his divinity perceived. Therefore here in Ps 73 it is more likely to be a characteristic of assimilation to the divinity. Like a mother with a child, God takes the psalmist by the hand (v. 23b) and guides him along the path of life by his 'counsel' (v. 24a) — the gift of law and grace, and thus leads him to a mysterious, yet nonetheless 'glorious' intimacy (v. 24b) — the faculty of experiencing his presence. It is *this* that constitutes the ultimate motive for the assurance that crowns the psalm.

The intellectual problem remains. If one goes by human experience and reason then God *is* alien, for who can find him in an absurd world where the just still suffer and the wicked still prosper? All that makes the situation tolerable in the context of Ps 73 is communion with God — and this, indeed, relegates the 'problem' to a position of little or no importance. One lives on this earth; one accepts the circumstances of the human condition bounded by death; but even in that arid human landscape God offers himself, and alone is desired — *for his own sake*, and not as a convenient *deus ex machina.*

What the psalmist perceives now, at the end of his traumatic intellectual journey, is the absolute human value of being possessed by God and possessing him. This is how the psalm closes — with a brief, intense declaration of faith re-discovered.

> But as for me it is good to be near God;
> I have made the Lord God my refuge,
> that I may tell of all thy works.
> (v. 28)

Precisely because it is in the society of the Lord that man finds his true fulfilment, his only 'good', the psalmist determines to cleave totally to God in this life. By doing this he transforms all earthly concepts of 'prosperity' and 'peace'.

Man may live hereafter (v. 24), or more likely he will die — but he has *already* transformed his mortal existence into the 'glory' of divine life.

Finding One's Rest in God

This was as far as the poet of Ps 73 could see, but several other psalms cast new light on the same problem by seeing it from another angle.

One such is Ps 84, a 'Song of Sion' that hails the glory of the temple and the divine presence. Words more than structure dominate the psalm and give it a special intensity of meaning. The first two verses hold the attention in a web of emotive terms:

How *lovely* is thy dwelling place,
O Lord of hosts!
My soul *longs*, yea, *faints*
for the courts of the Lord;
my *heart and flesh* sing for joy
to the living God.

The word 'lovely', in the Hebrew of v. 1, means 'beloved' and carries with it a definite overtone of the erotic, as a glance at the *Song of Solomon* 1,12–16 makes clear:

While the king was on his couch,
my nard gave forth its fragrance.
My beloved is to me a bag of myrrh,
that lies between my breasts.
My beloved is to me a cluster of henna blossoms
in the vineyards of Engedi.

Behold, you are beautiful, my love;
behold, you are beautiful;
your eyes are doves.
Behold, you are beautiful, my beloved,
truly lovely.
Our couch is green . . .

Here a related form of the word is used to marvellous effect, and indeed 'lovely' permeates Ps 84 with the same sensuous glow. The same is true of the verb 'longs', occurring in the reflexive form in v. 2a. 'Faints for', when it occurs with the preposition, as it does in this same verse, means 'to languish', and again is quasi-sensual terminology more fitting to an erotic poem like the *Canticle.* With the vocabulary of these two verses so heavily weighed towards the affective dimension of human life, the combination of 'heart and flesh' in v. 2b is suggestively emphatic.

It is clear that these two verses deal with a religious experience related to the presence of God in the temple, the 'courts of the Lord' being placed in apposition to the 'living God' himself. Given, then, the premise that in this context 'heart and flesh' signify man in his humanity we are led to infer that the *entire* person is caught up in the religious experience being spoken of here. Verse 2 is a recognition of the fact that man is an integrated entity, *and it is as such* (spiritual, material, affective) that he responds to God. The first two verses of Ps 84 employ the vocabulary of sexual love to communicate the profundity of the poet's experience. What is presented is an almost physical awareness, very human indeed, of the nearness of Yahweh. The author shows how the contemplation of God's 'dwelling place' produces an emotion akin to sensual desire; a desire for the life that has its source in God.

Now both this psalm and Ps 73 represent, in different ways, what might be called a 'temple experience' of God. But in fact in the psalter, as distinct from such *torah*-orientated books as *Leviticus* and *Deuteronomy*, the temple is not synonymous with the sacrifices offered there, or with the solely liturgical. Sacrifices are useful, it is recognized, even necessary to some extent, as a means of nourishing communion of life with God; but the psalms tend rather to emphasize the *internal* dimension, the interior attitude that accompanies a ritual act. After all, they point out, man cannot give anything to God that he has not first given to man. Ps 50,7–11 is emphatic about this:

> Hear, O my people, and I will speak,
> O Israel, I will testify against you.
> I am God, your God.
> I do not reprove you for your sacrifices;
> your burnt offerings are continually before me.
> I will accept no bull from your house,
> nor he-goat from your folds.
> For every beast of the forest is mine,
> the cattle on a thousand hills.
> I know all the birds of the air,
> and all that moves in the field is mine.

No. These are no more than the human language man uses to express his feelings towards God, as the same psalm explains in vv. 13–15:

> Do I eat the flesh of bulls,
> or drink the blood of goats?
> Offer to God a sacrifice of thanksgiving,
> and pay your vows to the Most High;
> and call upon me in the day of trouble;
> I will deliver you, and you shall glorify me.

Thus, as one reads the psalms an awareness grows that even when it is not possible to go to Jerusalem for a formal encounter with God one can nonetheless 'enter his presence' very effectively from afar:

> Why are you cast down, O my soul,
> and why are you disquieted within me?
> Hope in God; for I shall again praise him,
> my help and my God.

My soul is cast down within me,
therefore I remember thee
from the land of Jordan and of Hermon,
from Mount Mizar.
Deep calls to deep
at the thunder of thy cataracts;
all thy waves and thy billows have gone over me.
By day the Lord commands his steadfast love;
and at night his song is with me,
a prayer to the God of my life.
(Ps 42,5–8)

One meets the 'God of one's life' wherever one raises a 'song' or a 'prayer'.

Such a prayer is Ps 63. An observant reader immediately notes here an element that is unusual, perhaps unique for biblical prayer: there is no 'motive' clause; nothing is requested, nothing acknowledged with gratitude. One is left with a simple expression of disinterested love, an outpouring of personal joy that rises to moments of passion. The key theme is probably sacramental encounter with Yahweh in the temple liturgy (note v. 2), a meeting that infuses the extra-cultic life of the poet like a grace-note that lingers on the ear. Ps 63 can best be understood when viewed in the light of a personal encounter with God that leaves the individual with an unquenchable longing for a renewal of, a continuation of, the intimacy so experienced:

O God, thou art my God, I seek thee,
my soul thirsts for thee;
my flesh faints for thee,
as in a dry and weary land where no water is.
So I have looked upon thee in the sanctuary,
beholding thy power and glory.

These first two verses say it all. Once again, as in Ps 42, the contrast 'water/desert' emphasizes the emotional depth of the poetry. The point of balance between image and reality is found in v. 2 with the simple word 'so' — a link-word, a conjunctive. So intense was his desire (v. 1) that it could be satisfied only by his 'looking upon', that is meeting, God in the sanctuary (v. 2). This human desire brings about the theophany, which is then perceived to be valid even outside the actual liturgical service — for God himself is 'determined' in an analogous way by *his* longing for the psalmist:

Because thy *steadfast love* is better than life,
my lips will praise thee.
So I will bless thee as long as I live;
I will lift up my hands and call on thy name.
(vv. 3–4)

What the poet experiences is God's faithfulness, his divinity (or 'glory', v. 2b) as it is poured out in 'love' (v. 3a) on man. One might call it 'grace', without perhaps plumbing the full depth of the Hebrew term *hesed* (here translated as 'steadfast love'): gratuitous, unmerited, a gift to one who, as a sinner, is an 'enemy' to the divine. So overcome is the psalmist by this experience that he no longer conceives of *any* value in life that is not in some way representative of God's presence. *This* becomes the reality; all the rest is peripheral.

Verse 5 begins the poetic articulation of the experience, now as it were 'recollected in tranquillity'. This is the poet's real task — communicating his own experience to others. So what does he say?

My soul is feasted as with marrow and fat,
and my mouth praises thee with joyful lips,
when I think of thee upon my bed,
and meditate on thee in the watches of the night;
for thou hast been my help,
and in the shadow of thy wings I sing for joy.
(vv. 5–7)

The language of v. 5 is suggestive: his 'soul' (inner being) is *sated* (v. 5a); and so (v. 5b) he *praises* God. Indeed, the experience of union with God takes over the whole life of the psalmist — even those moments when, 'in the watches of the night' (v. 6b), he is to some extent under death's encroaching wing. What he first experienced in worship now permeates every situation of life; and given the temple context that must be theophanic presence. Thus the presence of God pushes its roots deep into the soil of human life, and in the rest of the psalm the author in fact tries to communicate this as he calls on a wide variety of symbols; 'helper' (v. 7), 'intimate companion' (v. 8), and, negatively, 'death' (v. 9), all sweep across the page in a flood of imagery as he tries to express the richness of the experience.

The Implications of Union with God

Psalm 1 is a different proposition to Ps 63 — calm, classical, academic in its treatment of life. It is a wisdom psalm, and probably represents the final point of view of the sages on the end of the wisdom project and so on the piety of the psalmist. As such, it was placed at the head of the collected psalter as a 'title page'. It begins, in sapiential style, with a formula that expresses a fact — not a hope, not a prayer, but a statement that a certain kind of person *is* 'happy', or blessed:

> Blessed is the man
>   who walks not in the counsel of the wicked,
> nor stands in the way of sinners,
>   nor sits in the seat of scoffers;
> (v. 1)

This type of person — known to his readers — is one who has consciously chosen the way of righteousness, and by this very fact is considered to be an authentic and humanly-fulfilled person. But it is clear that quite often in the experience of Israel, and of the psalmist, this cannot mean material prosperity or success, so once again (as in Ps 73) the reader is driven to ask — 'what is the nature of this felicity?'

The deliberate parallelism of the opening verses — antithetic parallelism presenting negative and positive portraits — forces the reader's attention on to v. 2, a positive statement.

> but his delight is in the law of the Lord,
>   and on his law he meditates day and night.

The single word 'law', perhaps, supplies the interpretive key. *Torah* as divine instruction for life suggests that here the psalmist is thinking of 'law' as the expression of God's own personality — the 'he' that God is in relation to the 'I' of the reader — and thus it becomes a catechesis for life, and life itself becomes a journey towards God. This is underlined by the grammatical form used in the Hebrew — a passage from Perfect verbal form in v. 1 to Imperfect in v. 2; so here one is dealing with a continuous, ongoing activity. It is against *this* background that the verb 'meditates' takes on a new significance. It implies more than speculation, more than passive 'contemplation' or acceptance. It has the significance of *life*, of something *lived*: as it were, one repeats the living, creative 'word' that is *torah*, and by speech enters into its reality, so that one 'speaks' it in a practical life-situation. But by far the most important word here — so surprising in its implications that it makes one stop and think again — is the verb 'delights in'. In Hebrew it has a precise and particular usage. In itself, and given the Old Testament context, it normally refers to the human affection that exists between man and woman, and therefore it is rich *in emotional* overtones. Semantically, in v. 2 it suggests the sensual delight that is found in sexual intercourse — indeed, the word is used in this sense in the *Song of Solomon*, for example. When followed, as it is here, by the preposition 'in' or 'towards', the object of the quasi-erotic sentiment can only be the '*torah* of Yahweh' understood as the person of the divinity manifested in his word. The 'beatitude' of the just consists solely in clinging to God with a personal, fully human passion, and in the movement of prayer experiencing an almost sensual delight in intercourse with him. And in fact this theology of union is echoed in the terminology of the last verse:

> for the Lord is knowing the way of the righteous,
> but the way of the wicked will perish.
> (v. 6)

So the psalm ends, as it began, in parallel; but this time positively, with the 'one who is considered blessed'. What is now his mark? 'God *is knowing* his way', and the verb expresses a knowledge born not of speculation but of personal experience. Given the careful structure of the psalm this must surely be taken as a deliberate contrast to vv. 4b–5:

> (The wicked) are like chaff which the wind drives away.
> Therefore the wicked will not stand in the judgement,
> nor sinners in the congregation of the righteous.

Recognition is in the sphere of human contact, and 'knowledge' is less cognitive than empirical, the result of human intercourse. God draws a certain type of person out from among others in order to communicate, to touch and to embrace. Ps 1 adds 'their way': their very life, daily life, is so formed that at each stage of it they experience divine contact.

Such a life, irrespective of biographical or social detail, is indeed 'blessed'.

Psalm 42–43 stands alongside of Ps 84 as a classic of this genre. When it is read as a unit one notices how a particular 'refrain' occurs three times: 42,5; 42,11 and 43,5:

Why are you cast down, O my soul,
and why are you disquieted within me?
Hope in God; for I shall again praise him,
my help and my God.

This serves as a concluding formula for three strophes that make up the prayer:

42,1–5: speaks of the psalmist's desire for God;
42,6–11: details his separation from God;
43,1–5: is a prayer for reconciliation.

The tone is set by the opening verses, which represent the inner attitude of the psalmist.

As a hart longs for flowing streams,
so longs my soul for thee, O God.
My soul thirsts for God, for the living God.
When shall I come and behold the face of God?
(vv. 1–2)

The poignance of the last line (and of v. 3) is due to the poet's exile from the temple (vv. 6–11). At first, it would seem, he believed he could slake his thirst for God only there, but the threefold refrain makes it clear that he gradually came to an awareness that it was not so. Thus it is not so much his nostalgia for the temple that is the dynamic of the psalm as his longing for God himself. And in fact this is confirmed by the superb imagery of v. 1. As it were, the psalmist's intense desire for God is verbalized into prayer and transformed into poetry: 'As a hart longs for flowing streams, so longs my soul for thee, O God'. For the hart water is a biological need, necessary to life itself. In an analogous way so is God for the psalmist. Two words now add intensity, transforming the metaphor into something of intimate significance: the hart 'longs for' water, and 'flowing water' what is more — an element that not only *gives* life *but is itself living.* Thus God, the secondary unit of the parallel, is both a source of life and is, himself, 'life' or 'living'. One imbibes one's nature from one's source of being, and so becomes in some way assimilated to that source in an identity of nature.

Testimony to Personal Relationship

This idea is expressed in more affective terms in Ps 27, which is clearly bi-partite — vv. 1–6 being an expression of faith and vv. 7–14 a 'lament'. Stylistically similar to Ps 23, the first six-verse section is almost confessional — a testimony to personal relationship with God who is spoken *of*, not *to* (the third person is used throughout this section). Like most biblical prayer it represents 'faith' in terms of a personal attitude to God based on experience — here the experience of temptation (vv. 2–3) and victory. For this reason it is a very mature testimony: the poet has seen life and can equate faith *with* life.

Verse 1 is clearly a personal 'credo' born of experience:

> The Lord is my light and my salvation;
> whom shall I fear?
> The Lord is the stronghold of my life;
> of whom shall I be afraid?

In the Old Testament 'light' is frequently a synonym for life, thus v. 1 is an exclusive statement — his reliance is on God *alone*, a question of 'I' and 'thou'. This sort of attitude is possible only to someone who has grown so close to God that nothing else matters — others, as it were, are peripheral; of no real relevance. Verse 2 confirms this view. There is no sign even of a request for help as the poet faces temptation; so close is his union with God that sin scarcely impinges. This dramatically sharpens the reader's perception as the focus of the psalm inevitably shifts to God, who now takes centre-stage as the poet meditates on him.

> One thing have I asked of the Lord,
> that will I seek after;
> that I may dwell in the house of the Lord
> all the days of my life,
> to behold the beauty of the Lord,
> and to inquire in his temple.
>
> For he will hide me in his shelter
> in the day of trouble;
> he will conceal me under the cover of his tent,
> he will set me high upon a rock.
>
> And now my head shall be lifted up
> above my enemies round about me;
> and I will offer in his tent
> sacrifices with shouts of joy;
> I will sing and make melody to the Lord.
> (vv. 4–6)

The psalmist opens himself to his 'Lord' (vv. 4–6) in an exclusive way, and places before the intrusive reader his own experience of union with God. As might be guessed from the first three verses, it is a very personal insight that is offered; indeed, it seems to be more a monologue than anything else — the poet musing to himself as if not even aware of an audience 'out there' listening.

The structure of this section is crucial. 'One thing' (v. 4) — the word dominates everything that follows, as the verse is structured around it. Verse 4a presents the one desire, communion with God, which is deepened *quantitatively* in v. 4b and *qualitatively* in v. 4c:

> *One thing alone* I seek!
> to dwell with God *all my life*;
> to *behold his beauty*.

The reason he wishes to 'dwell in God's house' (v. 4b) is scarcely liturgical; 'all the days of my life' reflects ethical rather than ritual qualities. Rather, his desire is that the intense 'closeness to God' that he experiences at moments during the liturgy may become his normal, everyday vital impulse. What this means on the theological level is that this desire for communion of being and life is *a gift of God*, not something acquired by human effort. God presenting himself in a liturgical theophany ('house of the Lord') himself awakes desire in the psalmist's heart. God seeks man; himself wishing for this relationship he arouses man. The idea is close to that expressed by Jeremiah, who saw his prophetic vocation in terms of God 'seducing' him in his innocence (Jer 20,7):

> O Lord, you have seduced me, and I was seduced;
> you are stronger than I, and you have prevailed.
> I have become a laughingstock all the day;
> everyone mocks me.

Unlike the prophet, the author of Ps 27 found this a happy seduction.

Verse 4c is the important statement, and merits special attention:

> to *gaze on* the *beauty* of Yahweh

A series of technical terms are used in the original Hebrew to load the statement. The word 'gaze' means to 'look at' something or someone, but when combined with the preposition 'in' or 'on' it assumes the significance of pleasure, carnal joy. One gets the impression that the author is sated with the richness of his encounter with holiness and thus finds *shalôm*, the fulness of human well-being. It has been suggested that a cognate form of the word used for 'beauty' in this verse is used in Canaanite literature for the beauty of the goddess Anath. If this is so, then the affective nature of the experience is highlighted even more. Indeed, vv. 5–6 tend to confirm the conjecture. Three terms — 'shelter', 'tent' and 'rock' — are used rather technically as metaphors of security, cohabitation and life (as has been seen in Ps 95 and Ps 15). If God *is* the real vital principle or impulse of his life then there are no longer *two* lives involved: the poet's own life has been merged into that of the divinity. In his prayer the psalmist has been 'seduced' by God and has surrendered his whole being in an act of mutual giving.

A New and Daring Concept of Intimacy with God

What decisively marks the piety of the psalms, particularly the wisdom psalms such as Ps 1 and Ps 73, is the fact that God *knows* one and so, logically, one can, by his gift, come to *know* him. In this relational context the verb has an existential connotation, suggesting that sort of knowledge that comes from experience rather than from speculation. It is frequently used in the Old Testament for the act of sexual intercourse, and so the poets could use it to forge a new and daring concept of intimacy with God.

The first glimpse of this 'new theology' was found in Ps 73 where the poet dealt with the discovery of God in a crisis that was both intellectual and emotional. Here the *person* was involved in the problem of God's silence, and the only answer given seems to have been intellectually inadequate. Yet in fact it is characteristic of the best of wisdom, and psalmic, piety, for it proposes an intense consciousness of the presence and approval of God that not so much solves the problem as renders it irrelevant. But this is no more than a first step in the theological adventure undertaken by the poets. Their perception of holiness as an experience of God that could be felt and understood led them to a more involved concept — that of 'delighting' in the Lord, or sharing an affective union with him. Possibly the finest flowering of this idea is found in Ps 1. This is a description of a certain kind of person — one who is 'blessed' in his intimacy with God, an intimacy that is described in terms reminiscent of human affection — that shared by two people on a sensitive level. Union has become a very subjective attitude, a strongly felt emotion for God as he manifests himself through his 'law', and a quasi-erotic delight in encounter with him.

These characteristics re-appear in a much more tautly-woven pattern in Ps 119. This is a classic psalm of the law, but it is also a wisdom psalm, and so the God-man relationship is more *intellectually* perceived. Here the concept of union with Yahweh occurs in confessional form — that is, as part of a creed, or formal declaration of religious faith. For this reason it has a particularly theological, and indeed cerebral, value, becoming an inalienable element of faith in the God of the Covenant. Ps 119 is concerned more strictly than any other psalm with the totality of revelation as doctrine. Yet what often breaks through the surface of the psalm is the idea of total *joy* one finds in this revelation, this expression of God's personhood which is a source of delight. All man's striving after holiness, or 'insight' as the poet sees it, is aimed at achieving union with God, which becomes the focus of one's emotional life as well as the goal of one's intellectual journey.

> Oh, how I love thy law!
>   It is my meditation all the day.
> Thy commandment makes me wiser than my enemies,
>   for it is ever with me.
> I have more understanding than all my teachers,
>   for thy testimonies are my meditation.
> I understand more than the aged,
>   for I keep thy precepts.
> I hold back my feet from every evil way,
>   in order to keep thy word.
> I do not turn aside from thy ordinances,
>   for thou hast taught me.
> How sweet are thy words to my taste,
>   sweeter than honey to my mouth!
> Through thy precepts I get understanding;
>   therefore I hate every false way.
>
> (vv. 97–104)

It is interesting to note that the most intimate expression of this human fulfilment occurs in such confessional, and therefore theological, forms. However, while they are personal statements they function on a more objective level as well. They are, in their way, paradigms: they stand as types of the 'saint', and while they remain they transcend human expression. It is for this reason that such ideas about the nature of union with God can be expressed only existentially — by means of poetry, or symbolic language. Indeed, the writers were forced to stretch language to its uttermost to communicate the depth of the experience. Words and images are packed together, layer upon layer and are used in ways that deliberately intensify the affective nature of the experience of God — 'thirst', 'delight', 'gaze upon', 'taste'. Normal language is not flexible enough to communicate the richness of the experience. What results from this 'theological adventurism' is a literary expression that is pregnant with a sense of psychological as well as spiritual fulfilment.

EPILOGUE

PRAYING THE POETRY OF THE PSALMS

One very real problem faces the reader of the psalms: they are poetry (and so subjective), while at the same time they are God's word to a third person beyond the poet. While they do not intend to teach anyone *about* God the reader does share in an experience of the divine that can be grasped intellectually. The reader may learn *by means of* a psalm. As one faces into the texts one must realize that they are verbalizations of a personal and vital experience, and can communicate that experience only through the alchemy of the poetic art. The function of poetry is to enable a writer to express the subjective dimension of an experience and thus render it possible for a reader to enter into that same experience and make it his own. It is always the communication of the impact life has on an individual, or in the case of the psalms the impact of God on an individual's life. Because of its immediacy to both writer and reader the language of poetry is always *evocative*; it opens up possibilities, and never directly indicates 'truths'. And it always raises questions, for the reader must consider to what extent his situation — and indeed his perception — is that of the author. 'How good God is to the upright' — Ps 73,1 is a credal statement, personalized by the poet. But what does it mean to a second person? How does that second person understand his *own* righteousness? And to what extent has he experienced the love of God *as a result of that righteousness*? 'The Lord is my shepherd' is the confident claim of Ps 23, and the poet builds up a theology of faith on that basis. But to a reader born in a city ghetto, what 'experience' can it possibly evoke? How can such a one ever identify? Only by a transposition of symbolism that respects both the language and the parameters of one's own experience.

The Function of Poetry

One might ask, 'why literary language in the first place? What end does it serve?' Effectively, it makes it possible to actualize an experience and make it objective, to the extent that it becomes immediately apprehensible on a subjective level. *His* experience is objectified so that it can become *mine.* Therefore, the individual re-experiencing, and not merely hearing about, the primary experience can assimilate it in a special way, and feel its immediacy and its impact. When a new generation, or a different language group, confronts a psalm, and its own experiences do not correspond to that of the poet, how is all of this possible? Only by the use of image, metaphor and symbol that have a common element with which the new reader can identify. Ps 23 places 'Lord' and 'shepherd' side by side as expressive of an experience of Yahweh. Here a modern reader may have no more than a partial experience of the idea contained in the image 'shepherd'. Therefore, he must not simply replace this image with an experience of his own. He must find the *significance* (and not merely the *meaning*) of this for an Israelite of the period, and transpose it to an image-evocation that corresponds to his own field of experience.

To do this he must ask three questions: what is its *objective* content (this he probably knows)?; what is its *subjective* content (its power to *evoke* a reaction) for the poet?; and finally what is its *subjective* content for the reader? While 'shepherd' *means* the same for anyone who knows the language, its *significance* for the author of Ps 23 and his Israelite reader was deeper and more emotive, conjuring up the hopes and expectations of the Davidic dynasty and the divine plan in the history of the people. So while at the first level, as an image of a caring God, one may readily identify, the subjective overtones may remain foreign. Therefore one must try to 'objectify' them and re-assimilate them at a new, personal level, so that what they signified for Israel may find its echo within the reader's field of experience.

Thus in the psalms the interweaving of author's tradition, poetic diction and reader's tradition makes particular demands on the interpreter. It goes without saying that he must respect the art of poetry — communication by means of symbolic language. But more: he must also understand the tradition in which the poet worked, the themes that played a major role in his belief and theology, the highlights of his history; and he must be capable of integrating all of this into his own religious perception of life. There is, as it were, an aid to all this immediately to hand — the framework of salvation-history.

The Framework of the Economy of Salvation

It has been observed that fundamental to the value of the psalms, and indeed to the whole of the Old Testament, is the unity of salvation-history. This serves as a point of reference to the reader's task, which is to link up the first stage of the divine design, which is found in the psalter, with his own 'today'. The Old Testament itself contains this progress from past to present, from the actuality of the psalmist to the contemporary situation of the reader. In the biblical tradition Ps 22 serves very well as an example of this — having been used centuries later by Christ as a prayer of his own 'today' (Mt 27,46).

> My God, my God, why have you forsaken me?
> Why are you so far from helping me,
> from the words of my groaning?

This first verse of Ps 22 was originally the reaction of an individual to what he felt was a totally undeserved suffering. Not an experience too many readers can claim for themselves. Yet at a later date someone could identify *because he felt himself to be in an analogous situation.* When this phenomenon is analyzed it is found to consist of two steps or stages of communication.

1) a subjective experience on the part of the author of Ps 22, being expressed in terms that make it objectively presentable, becomes applicable as

2) a subjective experience of the recitant, in a situation perceived to be analogous (Calvary).

This transposition is valid to the extent that the Calvary-experience can be identified with the Ps 22 experience. As Matthew sees it, this identity rests on the fact that the psalmist feels himself to be innocent, a servant of the divine purpose in history; a sufferer who ultimately is confident (from historical experience) that God is present to this event. And Christ can identify with all of this. Yet the analogy must be modified if it is to be re-actualized — modified to the extent that the Calvary-experience is *new*.

Psalm 114 presents a different problem of transposition.

When Israel went forth from Egypt,
the house of Jacob from a people of strange language,
Judah became his sanctuary,
Israel his dominion.
(vv. 1–2)

The Exodus event that is presented here, and which is clearly a historical experience, is apprehended anew and assimilated by means of a particular imagery in vv. 3–4:

The sea looked, and fled,
Jordan turned back.
The mountains skipped like rams,
the hills like lambs.

The mental picture conjured up by these words is unusual, perhaps even bizarre, but it has its own perceptual logic:

the sea receding — an evocation of all that Ex 14,21 and the Red Sea deliverance meant in terms of liberation: the flight of the 'oppressor' as God draws near the situation.

Jordan turning back — the significance derives from Josh 3,14 *and the way this tradition has been modified* by the author to suit a new situation in the life of God's people.

The inner nature of Exodus as liberation-act becomes once more a contemporary event in the psalmist's 'today', and provokes the use of the present-continuous in vv. 5–6, where new imagery carries the significance:

mountains leaping — an evocation of the Sinai theophany (Ex 19,16) communicated by a picture of the (improbable!) response of inanimate nature to theophany; a response that throws into relief the equally mind-boggling power and might of a God capable of producing such a phenomenon.

And why the interrogative form that dominates vv. 5–6? Why else but to involve the reader personally and immediately in nature's response to redemption?

It is in the nature of poetry to initiate a dialogue with a reader. Praying the psalms is just such an act — God offering himself through the sacrament of a human word, and man coming to meet him in that 'word'. The reader identifies with the first-hand experience of a poet and assimilates it. From this experience comes *knowledge*, and from knowledge, life.